12 Smart Tax Strategies For Retirees

A Comprehensive Guide to
Mastering Retirement Tax Strategy

By Jeff Weidner

Boom Retirement Solutions

Published by Jeff Weidner
Wake Forest, NC

Limited Liability and Disclaimer of Warranty:

Every effort has been made by the author and publisher to ensure the accuracy and completeness of this book. However, the publisher and author make no representations or warranties of any kind, express or implied, about the accuracy or completeness of the contents. They specifically disclaim all implied warranties of merchantability or fitness for a particular purpose.

The strategies and advice in this book may not be suitable for every situation. Neither the author nor the publisher shall be held liable for any loss of profit or other damages, including but not limited to special, incidental, consequential, or other damages arising out of the use or misuse of the information provided. Readers should consult with a qualified professional for personalized guidance.

First Edition
Published in Wake Forest, NC by Boom Retirement Solutions, 2025

Summary:

This guide provides 12 smart tax strategies every retiree should know to reduce tax liabilities, minimize Required Minimum Distributions (RMDs), and achieve lasting financial success in retirement.

Author: Jeff Weidner

Dedication

To all those approaching retirement, may you find the confidence and clarity to make the most of your retirement assets, reduce your taxes and create the retirement you deserve.

And to my family, whose support made this book possible.

Download your Free Book

https://books.jeffweidner.com/free

SCAN ME

DOWNLOAD FREE BOOK

Acknowledgments

Writing a book about Tax Strategies for Retirees that is both comprehensive and accessible requires the support and expertise of many individuals. I would like to express my deepest gratitude to:

My clients, whose questions and concerns helped shape the content of this book. Your trust in me to guide you through retirement planning decisions has been both a privilege and an inspiration.

The team at Boom Retirement Solutions, whose dedication to serving our clients with excellence provides the foundation for everything we do. Your commitment to helping people create secure retirement income strategies makes our work meaningful and impactful.

My mentors in the financial services industry taught me the importance of putting clients first and always continuing to learn. Your guidance has been invaluable in developing the expertise shared in these pages.

The editorial team, whose careful attention to detail helped ensure this complex subject matter is presented clearly and accurately. Your contributions have made this book more accessible and useful for readers.

My family, whose patience and support during the writing process made this book possible. Your encouragement kept me going through long hours of research and writing.

Finally, to you, the reader, for taking this important step toward understanding and maximizing your tax liabilities in retirement. Your commitment to creating a secure retirement future is admirable.

How to Use This Book

This book is designed to help you understand and maximize your specific tax strategies to reduce tax liability in retirement. Each chapter builds upon the previous one, providing a comprehensive understanding of the tax system and how it fits into your retirement planning.

Key Features:

Real-World Examples: Throughout the book, you'll find stories of real people facing common retirement tax decisions. These examples illustrate how different strategies can be applied to various situations.

Charts and Tables: Visual aids help clarify complex concepts and provide quick reference for important information.

Action Steps: Each chapter ends with specific steps you can take to apply what you've learned to your own situation.

Worksheets: The appendices contain practical worksheets to help you calculate your benefits, analyze your options, and create your retirement income plan.

Resource Directory: A comprehensive listing of additional resources and contact information is provided to help you access the support you need. Each has links to the specific IRS code and publications that we are referencing for additional information and clarification.

Table of Contents

INTRODUCTION: MASTERING YOUR RETIREMENT TAX STRATEGY

After decades of disciplined saving and careful planning, you've built substantial wealth for retirement. Yet many successful retirees discover that managing taxes during retirement can be even more complex than during their working years. This guide provides a comprehensive roadmap for retirees and soon-to-be retirees to navigate the intricate landscape of retirement taxation while maintaining full compliance with tax laws and regulations.

Why This Book Matters Now

The retirement landscape has transformed dramatically over the past few decades. The traditional model of relying on pension plans and Social Security has given way to a more complex system where retirees must actively manage multiple income sources and tax implications. Today's retirees face unique challenges:

- Required Minimum Distributions (RMDs) starting at age 73 (if born in 1959 or before, RMDs start at age 75 if born in 1960 or after)
- Potential changes in tax legislation
- Complex rules around Social Security taxation
- Medicare premium surcharges based on income
- Multiple streams of retirement income to manage

According to the Investment Company Institute's 2023 data, Americans held over $39 trillion in retirement assets, with a significant portion in tax-deferred accounts. This massive shift toward tax-deferred savings means that many retirees are facing what tax experts call a "tax time bomb" – accumulated wealth that has never been taxed but will be taxed as ordinary income when withdrawn.

Understanding Today's Retirement Reality

Meet Michael and Sarah Thompson, both aged 62, who recently retired with combined retirement assets of $2.1 million. Like many successful professionals, they spent years maximizing their 401(k) contributions and building their investment portfolio. However, they were surprised to learn that their tax burden might actually increase in retirement due to:

- Required distributions from their tax-deferred accounts
- Social Security benefit taxation
- Medicare premium surcharges
- Loss of common tax deductions they had while working

Their situation reflects a common challenge: while they succeeded in building substantial retirement assets, they now need strategies to manage the tax implications of accessing those assets.

Who This Book Is For

- This guide is specifically designed for:
- Retirees and pre-retirees aged 50-70

- Individuals with a net worth of $1 million or more (excluding primary residence)
- Those seeking to optimize their retirement tax situation legally and ethically
- People who want to understand how different retirement accounts and income sources affect their tax situation

Whether you're already retired or planning to retire within the next few years, the strategies in this book will help you make informed decisions about managing your retirement tax burden.

The Hidden Cost of Poor Tax Planning

Many retirees significantly underestimate the impact of taxes on their retirement income. A recent study by the American Institute of CPAs found that 57% of retirees wish they had been better prepared for taxes in retirement. Poor tax planning can lead to:

- Unnecessarily high tax bills that erode retirement savings
- Increased Medicare premiums due to higher reported income
- Greater taxation of Social Security benefits
- Reduced legacy for heirs
- Decreased retirement lifestyle quality

A New Approach to Retirement Tax Planning

This book presents a comprehensive framework for understanding and optimizing your retirement tax situation. Rather than focusing on aggressive tax avoidance schemes or questionable strategies, we emphasize legal, proven methods for managing your tax burden effectively.

What You'll Learn

Throughout this guide, you'll discover:

- How to structure retirement income to minimize taxes
- Strategies for managing Required Minimum Distributions
- Ways to reduce the taxation of Social Security benefits
- Methods for leveraging tax-advantaged investment vehicles
- Techniques for charitable giving that benefit both you and your chosen causes
- Approaches to estate planning that minimize tax impact on your heirs

How to Use This Book

Each chapter builds upon the previous ones, creating a comprehensive understanding of retirement tax strategy. You'll find:

- Clear explanations of complex concepts
- Real-world examples and case studies
- Action items for implementation
- References to current tax laws and regulations
- Guidelines for working with tax professionals

Important Considerations

While this guide provides valuable information and strategies, it's important to note that:

- Tax laws and regulations change frequently
- Individual circumstances vary significantly
- Professional guidance is often necessary for implementation
- Some strategies require long-term planning
- Not all approaches will be suitable for everyone

The Road Ahead

In the following chapters, we'll explore specific strategies and techniques for optimizing your retirement tax situation. From understanding the basics of retirement account taxation to implementing sophisticated tax-minimization strategies, this guide will provide you with the knowledge and tools needed to make informed decisions about your retirement finances.

Remember, the goal isn't to eliminate taxes entirely – that's neither realistic nor legal. Instead, we focus on optimizing your tax situation within the bounds of the law while ensuring you maintain the retirement lifestyle you've worked so hard to achieve.

Let's begin this journey toward a more tax-efficient retirement by exploring the fundamental concepts of retirement taxation in Chapter 1.

Disclaimer

The information presented in this book is for informational purposes only and is not intended to be, nor should it be considered, financial, tax, or legal advice. The strategies, case studies, and examples provided are illustrative and are based on hypothetical scenarios designed to demonstrate general principles. Actual results will vary based on individual circumstances, and the information may not apply to your specific situation.

Tax laws, thresholds, and financial regulations are subject to change and may differ by jurisdiction. While every effort has been made to ensure the accuracy and timeliness of the information presented, the authors and publishers cannot guarantee that it reflects the latest updates or individual applicability.

Readers are strongly encouraged to consult qualified professionals, such as a tax advisor, financial planner, or legal counsel, before implementing any strategies or making decisions based on the material in this book. These professionals can provide personalized guidance tailored to your unique financial and tax circumstances, ensuring compliance with current laws and regulations.

The authors and publishers disclaim all liability for any loss or damage resulting from the use of or reliance on this information. By using the information provided, you agree to hold the authors and publishers harmless from any and all claims or liabilities arising from decisions made based on this content.

For the most accurate and relevant advice, always refer to official sources, such as IRS publications or your financial institution, and seek personalized counsel from licensed professionals.

CHAPTER 1: THE FOUNDATION OF TAX-FREE RETIREMENT

Understanding the Modern Retirement Tax Landscape

The dream of a tax-efficient retirement often begins with a common assumption: your tax burden will naturally decrease once you stop working. Michael and Sarah Thompson held this belief firmly as they approached retirement with their carefully accumulated $2.1 million nest egg. Like many successful professionals, they had maximized their 401(k) contributions throughout their careers, diligently building their retirement savings. However, when they sat down with their financial advisor to plan their retirement distributions, they discovered a surprising reality that many retirees face.

"We always assumed we'd be in a lower tax bracket in retirement," Michael explains, leaning forward in his chair during our interview. "After all, we wouldn't be earning salaries anymore. But when we looked at how our retirement income would stack up—Social Security, Required Minimum Distributions, investment income—we realized we needed to think differently about taxes in retirement."

The Evolution of Retirement Taxation

The landscape of retirement taxation has undergone dramatic changes over the past few decades. Gone are the days when most Americans could rely primarily on pension plans and Social Security for their retirement income. In 1980, nearly 38% of private-sector workers could count on pension plans to provide guaranteed retirement income. Today, that number has plummeted to less than 15%, fundamentally changing how Americans must approach retirement planning and taxation.

This shift from pension-based to self-funded retirement has created new challenges that previous generations didn't face. Today's retirees must navigate a complex web of tax implications from multiple retirement accounts, each with its own rules and requirements. Adding to this complexity, increased longevity means retirement savings need to last longer than ever before. A retirement that spans 25 or 30 years isn't uncommon, making tax efficiency crucial for long-term financial success.

The Hidden Impact of Retirement Income Sources

Consider the experience of James and Linda Peterson, a couple who thought they had their retirement well planned. At age 65, they had accumulated $1.8 million across various accounts: $1.4 million in traditional IRAs, $200,000 in taxable investment accounts, and $200,000 in municipal bonds. They also expected to receive a combined $48,000 annually from Social Security. On paper, their situation looked solid.

However, the Petersons hadn't fully considered how Required Minimum Distributions would affect their tax situation at age 73. "The first time we calculated our required distributions, it was eye-opening," Linda recalls. "We realized these mandatory withdrawals would not only push us into a higher tax bracket but also increase our Medicare premiums and affect how much of our Social Security would be taxed. It felt like a domino effect we hadn't prepared for."

The Petersons' experience highlights a crucial reality of retirement taxation: it's not just about how much money you have, but how and when you access it. Different retirement income sources face different tax treatment, creating both challenges and opportunities for strategic planning.

The Three Pillars of Retirement Income

Understanding how different retirement income sources are taxed is crucial for effective planning. Think of your retirement income as a three-legged stool, with each leg representing a different type of account with its own tax treatment. Getting the balance right between these three sources can mean the difference between tax efficiency and unnecessary tax burden.

The first pillar consists of tax-deferred accounts like traditional IRAs and 401(k)s. These accounts have provided valuable tax deductions during your working years, but now they come with strings attached. Sarah Thompson discovered this when reviewing her retirement plans. "I had focused so much on the tax breaks while saving," she explains, "that I hadn't really thought about what it meant to have almost all our retirement money in tax-deferred accounts. Every dollar we withdraw will be taxed as ordinary income."

The second pillar includes tax-free accounts, primarily Roth IRAs and municipal bonds. These accounts offer unique advantages in retirement, as demonstrated by the Petersons' experience. After realizing the tax implications of their heavy reliance on traditional IRAs, they began a strategic conversion of some assets to Roth accounts. "Yes, we paid taxes on the conversions," James notes, "but now we have more control over our taxable income in retirement. When we need extra money for our grandson's college tuition or a special vacation, we can tap the Roth account without worrying about tax implications."

The third pillar encompasses taxable accounts, including individual investment accounts and real estate investments. While these accounts don't offer upfront tax advantages, they provide important flexibility in retirement. Capital gains rates on long-term investments are typically lower than ordinary income tax rates, and you have more control over when to realize gains or losses.

The Social Security Tax Surprise

One of the most misunderstood aspects of retirement taxation involves Social Security benefits. Many retirees are shocked to learn that their Social Security benefits might be taxed at all, let alone that up to 85% of these benefits could be subject to taxation. The Thompsons encountered this revelation during their retirement planning.

"We had calculated our retirement income based on our full Social Security benefit," Michael shares. "Nobody had ever explained to us that earning too much from other sources could make our Social Security benefits taxable. It felt like we were being penalized for saving diligently throughout our careers."

The taxation of Social Security benefits operates on a unique formula that can create what tax professionals call the "tax torpedo." A "tax torpedo" is a sudden increase in marginal tax rates caused by the taxation of Social Security benefits when other income crosses certain thresholds. As your income from other sources increases, more of your Social Security benefits become subject to taxation. This can effectively create a marginal tax rate higher than your tax bracket would suggest.

Consider a married couple receiving $36,000 annually in Social Security benefits. If their other income sources push them over certain thresholds, they might suddenly find 85% of their Social Security benefits subject to taxation. This could mean an additional $30,600 of taxable income they hadn't planned for.

2025 IRMAA Income Brackets and Premium Adjustments

Filing Status	Part B Premium (Monthly)	Part D Premium Adjustment
Individual < $103,000	$164.90	$0.00
Individual 103, 000 – 129,000	$230.80	$12.20
Individual 129, 001 – 161,000	$329.70	$31.50
Individual 161, 001 – 500,000	$428.60	$50.70
Individual > $500,000	$527.50	$70.00
Married Filing Jointly < $206,000	$164.90	$0.00
Married 206, 000 – 258,000	$230.80	$12.20
Married 258, 001 – 322,000	$329.70	$31.50
Married 322, 001 – 750,000	$428.60	$50.70
Married > $750,000	$527.50	$70.00

The Medicare Premium Connection

Adding another layer of complexity to retirement tax planning is the impact on Medicare premiums. Linda Peterson learned this lesson when their Required Minimum Distributions began. "We knew our Medicare premiums weren't fixed," she explains, "but we didn't realize they were tied to our income from two years prior. By the time we understood the connection, it was too late to prevent a significant increase in our healthcare costs."

The Income-Related Monthly Adjustment Amount (IRMAA) can substantially increase Medicare premiums based on your Modified Adjusted Gross Income. For 2024, married couples with MAGI exceeding $194,000 face higher premiums, with additional increases at various income thresholds. This creates a domino effect: higher taxable income leads to higher Medicare premiums, effectively creating another form of taxation.

Building a Strategic Approach

Understanding these complex interactions between different types of income and their tax implications is just the first step. The key is developing a strategic approach that considers all these factors together. The Petersons, after their initial wake-up call, worked with their financial advisor to create a comprehensive plan.

Their strategy began with a careful analysis of their various income sources and potential tax implications. They started Roth conversions during their early retirement years, when their taxable income was lower. They also coordinated their Social Security claiming strategy with their other income sources, ultimately deciding to delay benefits until age 70 to maximize their lifetime benefits while managing their tax situation.

"It's like putting together a puzzle," James reflects. "Each piece—Social Security, retirement account withdrawals, investment income—needs to fit together in a way that minimizes taxes while providing the income we need. And the picture keeps changing as tax laws and our needs evolve."

State Tax Considerations: An Often-Overlooked Factor

While federal tax planning often takes center stage, state taxation can significantly impact your retirement income. The Thompsons discovered this while considering a move in retirement. "We'd always dreamed of moving closer to our grandchildren in Florida," Sarah explains. "When we looked into the tax implications, we realized that moving from our high-tax state could save us thousands each year in retirement taxes."

State taxation of retirement income varies dramatically across the country. Some states, like California, tax nearly all forms of retirement income at rates that can exceed 13%. Others, like Florida and Texas, have no state income tax at all. Then there are states like Illinois and Pennsylvania that exempt most retirement income from taxation while still taxing other types of income.

The Petersons faced this decision when considering a move from New Jersey to Pennsylvania. "We discovered that Pennsylvania doesn't tax retirement account withdrawals or Social Security benefits," Linda shares. "But we had to consider other factors too, like property taxes and the cost of living. It's not just about income taxes."

The Professional Team Approach

Creating an effective retirement tax strategy isn't a solo endeavor. The most successful retirees build a team of professionals who work together to optimize their retirement tax situation. Michael Thompson initially resisted this approach, thinking he could manage everything himself. "I've always been good with numbers," he admits, "but when I saw how the various parts of our retirement tax picture interacted, I realized we needed professional help."

The Thompsons assembled a team consisting of a tax professional, a financial advisor, and an estate planning attorney. Each professional brought specific expertise that, when combined, created a comprehensive approach to their retirement tax planning. Their tax professional helped them understand the implications of different withdrawal strategies. Their financial advisor ensured their investment approach aligned with their tax strategy. Their estate planning attorney helped them structure their legacy plans in a tax-efficient manner.

"What surprised us most," Sarah notes, "was how often these professionals needed to coordinate with each other. Our retirement specialist would suggest a Roth conversion strategy, our tax professional would analyze the tax implications, and our estate planning attorney would advise how it fit into our legacy goals. It was like watching a well-orchestrated dance."

Roth conversions can be a powerful strategy for achieving tax-free retirement income, but they must be carefully planned. Large conversions in a single year can push you into a higher tax bracket, increase the taxation of your Social Security benefits, or trigger Medicare IRMAA surcharges, resulting in higher premiums. To minimize these risks, consider spreading conversions over several years and staying within tax brackets or income thresholds that align with your retirement goals. Always consult a tax professional to determine the optimal conversion strategy for your situation.

Looking Forward: The Importance of Flexibility

One crucial lesson both the Thompsons and Petersons learned is the importance of building flexibility into their retirement tax strategy. Tax laws change, personal circumstances evolve, and what works today might need adjustment tomorrow. James Peterson emphasizes this point: "We learned to think of our retirement tax strategy as a living document, not a set-it-and-forget-it plan."

This flexibility proved valuable when the SECURE Act changed the rules for inherited IRAs in 2019. The Petersons had originally planned to stretch their IRA distributions over their children's lifetimes as a tax-efficient inheritance strategy. When the law changed to require most non-spouse beneficiaries to withdraw inherited IRA funds within 10 years, they adjusted their strategy, incorporating more Roth conversions to reduce their children's future tax burden.

Creating Your Foundation

As we wrap up this foundational chapter, it's important to understand that creating a tax-efficient retirement isn't about finding a magic formula or quick fix. Instead, it's about building a solid foundation of knowledge and making informed decisions based on your specific situation.

The Thompsons' journey illustrates this perfectly. "We started by really understanding our current situation," Michael explains. "We gathered all our account statements, projected our future income needs, and took time to learn about how different types of retirement income are taxed. Only then did we start making decisions about specific strategies."

Linda Peterson adds a final piece of wisdom from their experience: "Don't get overwhelmed trying to implement everything at once. Start with understanding your situation and making the most pressing decisions first. Then build on that foundation over time."

As we move into the next chapter on Fixed Indexed Annuities, remember that every strategy we discuss will build upon this foundational understanding of retirement taxation. The clearer your grasp of these basics, the better equipped you'll be to make informed decisions about more sophisticated tax-planning strategies.

Building on Your Foundation: A Preview of What's Ahead

As we conclude our discussion of retirement tax fundamentals, let's return to the Thompsons' story one final time. After getting a firm grasp on their retirement tax situation, Michael and Sarah faced a new challenge: how to create reliable, tax-efficient income throughout their retirement years.

"Understanding the basics was essential," Sarah reflects, "but we still needed to figure out how to put it all together into a working strategy. That's when our advisor introduced us to the concept of Fixed Indexed Annuities as one potential tool in our retirement toolkit."

The Thompsons' experience mirrors that of many retirees who, after understanding the fundamental tax challenges they face, begin searching for specific strategies to address them. Their journey leads us naturally into our next chapter, where we'll explore how Fixed Indexed Annuities can play a role in creating tax-efficient retirement income.

Think of what we've learned in this chapter as the foundation of a house. We've laid down solid concrete by understanding:

- How different retirement accounts are taxed
- The impact of Social Security taxation
- The role of Required Minimum Distributions
- The importance of state tax considerations
- The value of professional guidance

Now, we're ready to start building the first floor of our tax-efficient retirement home. In Chapter 2, we'll examine how Fixed Indexed Annuities can serve as structural support for your retirement income strategy. You'll learn how these financial tools can help address some of the tax challenges we've discussed, while potentially providing other benefits for your retirement planning.

James Peterson, who we'll continue following in the next chapter, offers this perspective: "Once we understood the tax challenges we faced, we became more open to exploring different solutions. Fixed Indexed Annuities weren't something we'd seriously considered before, but understanding our tax situation helped us see their potential role in our overall plan."

As we move forward, keep in mind that every strategy we discuss should align with the foundational principles we've covered here. Just as a house needs a solid foundation to support everything built upon it, your understanding of basic retirement taxation will help you better evaluate and implement more sophisticated strategies.

In Chapter 2, we'll explore:

- How Fixed Indexed Annuities can complement your existing retirement accounts
- Ways to potentially reduce your taxable income using these tools
- Strategies for coordinating annuity income with Social Security benefits
- Methods for managing Required Minimum Distributions
- Approaches to creating tax-efficient legacy plans

The Thompsons' story will continue, along with other real-world examples, as we examine how Fixed Indexed Annuities might fit into your retirement tax strategy. Remember, there's no one-size-fits-all solution, but understanding all your options is crucial for making informed decisions about your retirement future.

Turn the page to begin exploring how Fixed Indexed Annuities might play a role in your tax-efficient retirement strategy.

References

Introduction & Chapter 1: Foundation of Tax-Free Retirement

Publication 554: Tax Guide for Seniors

https://www.irs.gov/forms-pubs/about-publication-554

Publication 915: Social Security and Equivalent Railroad Retirement Benefits

https://www.irs.gov/forms-pubs/about-publication-915

Publication 590-B: Distributions from Individual Retirement Arrangements (IRAs)

https://www.irs.gov/forms-pubs/about-publication-590b

Publication 575: Pension and Annuity Income

https://www.irs.gov/forms-pubs/about-publication-575

CHAPTER 2: STRATEGIC USE OF FIXED INDEXED ANNUITIES

Creating Tax-Efficient Income in Retirement

When Michael and Sarah Thompson first heard the term "Fixed Indexed Annuity" during a meeting with their Retirement Specialist, their initial reaction was skepticism. Like many retirees, they had heard conflicting information about annuities and weren't sure if such products would fit into their retirement strategy.

"I remember sitting there thinking, 'Isn't this just another complex financial product?'" Michael recalls, smiling at the memory. "But when our advisor explained how it could help address some of the tax challenges we discussed in our previous meetings, I realized we needed to keep an open mind."

Understanding Fixed Indexed Annuities: Beyond the Basics

To appreciate how Fixed Indexed Annuities (FIAs) can enhance your retirement tax strategy, it's helpful to first understand what makes them unique. Think of an FIA as a hybrid financial tool that combines elements of both traditional fixed annuities and market-linked investments, but with its own distinct characteristics.

James Peterson, whom we met in our previous chapter, explains his initial understanding this way: "Our specialist described it as having three key features: tax-deferred growth potential, protection from market losses, and the ability to create guaranteed income. But what really caught our attention was how it could help manage our tax situation in retirement."

The tax treatment of Fixed Indexed Annuities plays a crucial role in their appeal to retirees. Unlike traditional investment accounts where you pay taxes on gains each year, the growth in an FIA remains tax-deferred until you begin taking withdrawals. This feature proved particularly valuable for the Thompsons as they sought ways to control their taxable income in retirement.

Additionally, many FIA carriers offer up front bonuses and indexed returns which can be used to pay the taxes due when you perform the Roth conversion. The bonuses range are in the 5% to 20% range and are added to your account balance at the beginning of the contract term. This allowed the Thompsons to use the bonus to pay the taxes instead of using money from their checking or savings account.

The Harrison Strategy: A Real-World Example

Consider the experience of Robert and Patricia Harrison, a couple who successfully integrated FIAs into their retirement tax strategy. At age 65, the Harrisons found themselves in a common situation: they had accumulated substantial wealth in tax-deferred accounts but were concerned about future Required Minimum Distributions (RMDs) pushing them into higher tax brackets.

"We had about $1.8 million in traditional IRAs," Patricia explains, sitting in their sun-filled Florida living room. "Our financial advisor helped us understand that when RMDs kicked in at 73, we'd be forced to withdraw more than we needed, potentially pushing us into a higher tax bracket and increasing our Medicare premiums."

Working with their advisor, the Harrisons developed a multi-faceted strategy using Fixed Indexed Annuities:

First, they used some of their after-tax savings to purchase an FIA with an income rider. "This gave us a predictable income stream that we could count on," Robert notes. "More importantly, since we purchased it with after-tax money, only the earnings portion of our withdrawals would be taxable, which helped us manage our tax bracket."

Next, they used a portion of their IRA funds to purchase a qualified FIA. "The idea here," Patricia continues, "was to diversify how our retirement money was invested while maintaining the tax-deferral benefits we already had in our IRA. The guaranteed income features gave us more certainty about our future RMDs."

Understanding the Tax Advantages Through Real Experience

The Harrisons' strategy demonstrates one approach to using FIAs, but let's dive deeper into how these products can work in different situations. Linda Peterson, who we met earlier, shares her family's different approach to using Fixed Indexed Annuities.

"We were primarily concerned about market volatility affecting our tax planning," Linda explains, seated in her home office surrounded by carefully organized financial documents. "We had experienced how market downturns could disrupt our tax strategy by forcing us to sell investments at inopportune times to generate needed income. We wanted more predictability."

The Petersons worked with their advisor to implement what they call their "three-bucket strategy":

Bucket one consisted of their "immediate needs" money, held in traditional savings accounts. Bucket two contained their Fixed Indexed Annuity, designed to provide "reliable income" for years 5-15 of retirement. Bucket three held their "longer-term growth" investments.

"The beauty of this arrangement," James Peterson adds, "is how it helps us manage our tax situation. We know exactly how much taxable income our FIA will generate each year, making it easier to plan other withdrawals and manage our tax brackets."

The Power of Tax Deferral: A Closer Look

To understand why tax deferral matters so much in retirement planning, let's return to the Thompson family's experience. Michael and Sarah discovered that tax deferral in an FIA works differently from their traditional IRA.

"What caught our attention," Sarah explains, "was learning that when we eventually took withdrawals from our non-qualified FIA, we wouldn't owe taxes on our entire withdrawal. Instead, a portion would be considered a return of our original investment and therefore not taxable."

This concept, known as the exclusion ratio, became a valuable tool in their tax planning. Here's how it worked in their situation:

The Thompsons purchased a $500,000 FIA with after-tax money. When they began taking income, their insurance company calculated that 80% of each payment would be considered return of principal (not taxable) and 20% would be considered earnings (taxable). This meant that on a $40,000 annual withdrawal, only $8,000 would be added to their taxable income for the year.

"This was a game-changer for us," Michael notes. "It gave us more control over our taxable income than we had with our traditional IRA withdrawals, where every dollar is taxed as ordinary income."

Coordinating FIAs with Social Security Benefits

Patricia Harrison discovered another valuable aspect of FIAs when coordinating her retirement income with Social Security benefits. "Our advisor showed us how we could use our FIA income to delay claiming Social Security until age 70," she shares. "This not only increased our eventual Social Security benefit but also gave us more control over how much of our Social Security would be taxed once we started receiving it."

This strategy worked because the Harrisons could rely on their FIA income during the years between their retirement and age 70, when they planned to claim Social Security. By delaying Social Security, they:

- Increased their lifetime Social Security benefit by 32%

- Created more flexibility in managing their taxable income

- Reduced the potential taxation of their Social Security benefits

- Maintained their desired lifestyle during the delay period

"Looking back," Robert reflects, "using the FIA as a bridge to delayed Social Security benefits was one of our smartest moves. It not only increased our guaranteed lifetime income but also gave us more tax planning flexibility throughout retirement."

Addressing Common Concerns

The Thompsons, like many retirees considering FIAs, initially had concerns about committing money to an annuity. "We worried about losing access to our money," Michael admits. "But we learned that many FIAs offer liquidity features that allow you to access your funds if needed, though this needs to be planned carefully to avoid tax implications."

Planning for the Next Generation: The Legacy Consideration

The topic of leaving money to their children was particularly important to Sarah Thompson. "We wanted to create tax-efficient income for ourselves, but not at the expense of our legacy plans," she explains. "Understanding how FIAs fit into inheritance planning became a crucial part of our decision-making process."

Working with their estate planning attorney, the Thompsons learned that FIAs offer several options for legacy planning. They chose to structure their FIA with a death benefit rider that would protect their initial investment for their children. More importantly, they discovered how the tax treatment of inherited annuities could benefit their heirs.

"What we found particularly valuable," Michael adds, "was learning how our beneficiaries could choose to receive the death benefit either as a lump sum or spread out over time. This flexibility could help them manage their own tax situations when they inherit."

Coordinating FIAs with Required Minimum Distributions

James and Linda Peterson faced a different challenge: coordinating their FIA strategy with Required Minimum

Distributions from their traditional IRAs. Their solution demonstrates the importance of timing in FIA planning.

"We realized that our RMDs would start forcing taxable distributions at age 73," Linda explains, spreading out their financial planning calendar on their dining room table. "So we worked backwards from there to create a strategy that made sense."

The Petersons' approach involved two types of FIAs:

1. A non-qualified annuity purchased with after-tax money to provide supplemental income before RMDs began

2. A qualified annuity within their IRA that was specifically designed to help satisfy their RMD requirements

"The key was understanding how these different types of annuities would be taxed," James notes. "Our qualified annuity distributions would be fully taxable, just like any IRA withdrawal, but they would satisfy our RMD requirements. Meanwhile, our non-qualified annuity provided tax-advantaged income that helped us manage our tax bracket."

Real-World Implementation: The First Five Years

Robert Harrison shares his family's experience during the crucial first five years after implementing their FIA strategy:

"The transition wasn't just about buying an annuity and being done with it. We had to adjust our overall financial approach."

The Harrisons' five-year journey reveals important lessons about implementing an FIA strategy:

Year One: They focused on understanding their income rider and how withdrawals would be taxed. "We actually took less than we could have," Patricia remembers, "because we wanted to be conservative while we learned the ins and outs of our contract."

Year Two: They coordinated their FIA income with other investments to optimize their tax situation. This included timing withdrawals from different accounts to stay within their target tax bracket.

Year Three: They faced their first major market downturn since purchasing their FIA. "That's when we really appreciated the protection features," Robert notes. "While our other investments dropped in value, our FIA income remained stable, helping us avoid selling investments at low prices to generate income."

Year Four: They began using their FIA's inflation adjustment feature to help maintain purchasing power. "This was a key benefit we hadn't fully appreciated when we first purchased the contract," Patricia explains.

Year Five: They reviewed and adjusted their beneficiary designations to optimize the inheritance tax treatment for their children. "We learned that small details in how you structure beneficiary designations can make a big difference in how inherited annuities are taxed," Robert shares.

Fine-Tuning the Strategy: Lessons Learned

Understand the tax treatment for each account type

- Tax-deferred (IRA/401(k)): Fully taxable as ordinary income.
- Tax-free (Roth IRA): No taxes on withdrawals.
- Taxable (municipal bonds): Interest is often state and federal tax-exempt but could impact provisional income.

The Thompsons' experience during their implementation phase revealed important insights about integrating FIAs into a broader retirement strategy. "We learned that it's not just about the FIA itself," Sarah reflects, "but how it works with everything else in your retirement plan."

Learning from Experience: Common Challenges and Solutions

One afternoon, sitting in their favorite local coffee shop, Michael and Sarah Thompson shared some of the challenges they encountered with their FIA strategy. "Our biggest learning curve wasn't understanding the product itself," Michael explains, stirring his coffee thoughtfully. "It was figuring out how to integrate it with our other retirement income sources."

The Thompsons discovered that timing withdrawals from different accounts required careful planning. Sarah pulls out a small notebook where she tracks their income sources. "We learned to coordinate our FIA withdrawals with our other investment income to stay within our target tax bracket. Some months, we take more from our FIA; other months, we rely more heavily on our taxable accounts."

This flexibility proved especially valuable when unexpected expenses arose. Last year, when their daughter needed help with a down payment on her first home, they were able to adjust their withdrawal strategy without triggering unnecessary taxes. "Having multiple income sources, each with different tax treatment, gives us options we wouldn't have had otherwise," Sarah notes.

The Role of Market Conditions

The Petersons' experience highlights another important aspect of FIA strategy: how market conditions affect decision-making. Linda Peterson remembers the market volatility they experienced in their first years of retirement.

"We had friends who were forced to sell investments at losses to generate income. Meanwhile, our FIA provided steady income regardless of market conditions."

James adds an important perspective: "But you have to understand what you're giving up for that security. During strong market years, our FIA credits were capped. The key is finding the right balance for your situation."

Their solution was to use their FIA as part of a broader strategy:

- The FIA provided guaranteed income for essential expenses
- Their stock portfolio offered growth potential for longer-term needs
- Their bond holdings provided additional stability and income
- Cash reserves gave them flexibility for unexpected needs

Adapting to Life Changes

Robert and Patricia Harrison's experience demonstrates how FIA strategies often need adjustment as life circumstances change. Three years into their retirement, they faced an unexpected challenge when Robert's mother needed assisted living care.

"Suddenly, we needed to help with her care expenses while protecting our own retirement security," Patricia explains. "Having the guaranteed income from our FIA gave us the confidence to use other assets to help with her care."

The Harrisons worked with their advisor to adjust their strategy:

1. They maintained their existing FIA withdrawals for basic expenses
2. They sold some taxable investments for additional cash flow
3. They coordinated with Robert's siblings to share care costs
4. They explored long-term care options for themselves

"This experience taught us the importance of building flexibility into our retirement income plan," Robert reflects. "Having different types of assets and income sources helped us adapt to changing needs."

The Evolution of Understanding

Sarah Thompson's perspective on their FIA strategy evolved significantly over time. "At first, we saw our FIA primarily as a tax management tool," she explains. "But over the years, we've come to appreciate its other benefits – particularly the peace of mind it provides."

The Thompsons now view their FIA as playing multiple roles in their retirement:

- Providing reliable income they can't outlive
- Offering tax-advantaged growth potential
- Protecting a portion of their retirement assets from market risk
- Creating a legacy for their children
- Simplifying their financial management as they age

"One aspect we didn't fully appreciate initially," Michael adds, "was how our FIA would simplify our financial management as we get older. Knowing that a portion of our income is guaranteed and automatically deposited each month reduces the complexity of our retirement planning."

The Bigger Picture: Integrating FIAs into Your Retirement Story

As we conclude our exploration of Fixed Indexed Annuities, it's worth reflecting on how our featured families have used these tools to enhance their retirement security. The Thompsons, Petersons, and Harrisons each found different ways to incorporate FIAs into their retirement strategies, demonstrating that there's no one-size-fits-all approach.

"Looking back," Sarah Thompson reflects, sitting in her garden where she now spends many relaxed afternoons, "our FIA decision wasn't just about tax efficiency. It was about creating certainty in an uncertain world. That certainty has given us the confidence to truly enjoy our retirement."

James Peterson offers a practical perspective from five years into their strategy: "The key is understanding that an FIA is just one tool in your retirement toolkit. It's not about putting all your eggs in one basket, but rather about using each tool for what it does best."

The Harrisons, now helping their adult children plan for their own retirement, share a final insight. "We've learned that retirement planning is a journey, not a destination," Robert explains. "Our FIA provided a foundation of reliable income that let us adapt to life's changes without constant worry about market fluctuations or tax implications."

Looking Ahead

As we move into our next chapter on turning hobbies into tax-advantaged businesses, remember that each strategy we discuss builds upon the others. Just as the families we've met used FIAs as part of their larger retirement picture, we'll explore how developing a business around your passions can add another dimension to your retirement tax planning.

Patricia Harrison, who recently started selling her artwork at local galleries, gives us a perfect transition to our next topic: "The guaranteed income from our FIA gave me the confidence to explore my passion for painting without worrying about whether it would generate immediate income. Now, three years later, my art business has become both a joy and a tax-efficient part of our retirement plan."

Remember these key takeaways as we move forward:

- FIAs can provide tax-advantaged growth and income
- Integration with other retirement accounts and income sources is crucial
- Flexibility in implementation allows adaptation to changing circumstances
- Professional guidance helps optimize tax and income benefits
- Regular strategy reviews ensure continued alignment with your goals

Turn the page to discover how turning your hobby into a business might add another dimension to your retirement tax strategy, potentially working alongside the FIA and other approaches we've discussed to create a more tax-efficient retirement.

References

Chapter 2: Fixed Indexed Annuities
Publication 939: General Rule for Pensions and Annuities

https://www.irs.gov/forms-pubs/about-publication-939

Publication 575: Pension and Annuity Income
https://www.irs.gov/forms-pubs/about-publication-575

CHAPTER 3: TURN YOUR HOBBY INTO A BUSINESS

Creating Tax Advantages Through Your Passions

Patricia Harrison never imagined her lifelong love of painting would become a key part of her retirement tax strategy. "I always thought of my art as just a hobby," she says, standing in her sun-filled home studio, surrounded by canvases in various stages of completion. "The idea that it could help us manage our taxes in retirement seemed far-fetched at first."

Yet Patricia's journey from hobbyist to successful business owner illustrates a powerful strategy for retirees looking to optimize their tax situation while doing something they love. Her story, along with others we'll meet in this chapter, demonstrates how turning a hobby into a legitimate business can create valuable tax advantages while adding purpose and joy to retirement.

The Art of Business: Patricia's Journey

When Patricia first considered selling her artwork, she approached it casually, occasionally participating in local art fairs. However, her financial advisor saw greater potential – not just for income, but for tax advantages that could complement the retirement strategy we explored in earlier chapters.

"My advisor explained that as a hobby, my art expenses were essentially non-deductible," Patricia recalls. "But as a legitimate business, these same expenses could become tax deductions. That got my attention."

Working with her tax professional, Patricia took systematic steps to transform her hobby into a business:

1. Created a separate business checking account
2. Developed a formal business plan
3. Established proper recordkeeping systems
4. Started marketing her work professionally
5. Tracked all business-related expenses

"The transformation wasn't just about tax benefits," she explains. "It changed how I approached my art. I became more focused, more professional. And yes, the tax advantages have been significant."

Understanding the Hobby-to-Business Transition

Michael Thompson, whom we met in previous chapters, found his own path to business ownership through his woodworking hobby. "After retiring from my corporate job, I spent more time in my workshop," he shares. "When neighbors started asking if they could buy my pieces, I realized I might have an opportunity."

However, Michael learned that the IRS looks carefully at the distinction between hobbies and businesses. His tax advisor explained that the "profit motive" test would be crucial for his woodworking enterprise to qualify as a legitimate business.

"I had to prove this wasn't just a hobby where I occasionally sold things," Michael explains. "The IRS wants to see that you're operating like a real business, with the intention of making a profit. That meant changing how I approached everything."

The Nine Factors: Making the IRS Happy

The **nine factors** the IRS uses to determine if an activity qualifies as a business:

1. The manner in which the taxpayer carries out the activity.
2. The expertise of the taxpayer or their advisers.

3. The time and effort expended in carrying out the activity.
4. The expectation that assets used in the activity may appreciate in value.
5. The success of the taxpayer in carrying out other similar or dissimilar activities.
6. The taxpayer's history of income or losses with respect to the activity.
7. The amount of occasional profits, if any, which are earned.
8. The financial status of the taxpayer.
9. Elements of personal pleasure or recreation associated with the activity.

Sarah Chen, a retired accountant who now consults with retirees transitioning hobbies to businesses, explains the nine factors the IRS considers when determining if an activity is a legitimate business:

"Think of it as a story you're telling through your actions and records," Sarah suggests. "Every business decision should help demonstrate that you're serious about profitability."

Sarah Chen shares the key factors through the experience of her clients, the Thompsons and others who have successfully made the transition:

"The first factor is how you carry out the activity," she explains. "Michael's woodworking business is a perfect example. He maintains detailed records, has a separate business bank account, and creates professional invoices for every sale. These aren't just good business practices – they demonstrate profitability intention to the IRS."

Michael nods in agreement. "I learned to track everything – not just sales and expenses, but also time spent on different projects, marketing efforts, and customer feedback. This documentation has been invaluable for both business decisions and tax purposes."

Building a Professional Foundation

Patricia Harrison's art business demonstrates another crucial aspect: expertise in the field. "I didn't just rely on my years of painting experience," she explains. "I took business courses specifically for artists, joined professional associations, and sought mentoring from successful gallery owners. This showed I was serious about making my art business successful."

The Harrisons worked with their tax advisor to create a business structure that would optimize their tax situation. They considered several options:

- Sole Proprietorship

- Limited Liability Company (LLC)
- S-Corporation

"We ultimately chose an LLC taxed as a sole proprietorship," Patricia shares. "It gave us liability protection while keeping our tax reporting relatively simple. Plus, it allowed us to easily deduct legitimate business expenses."

Understanding Business Deductions

One of the most significant advantages of transitioning from hobby to business is the ability to deduct ordinary and necessary business expenses. James Peterson, who turned his photography hobby into a thriving business, explains how this works in practice.

"As a hobby photographer, I couldn't deduct the cost of my cameras, travel to photo locations, or editing software," James says. "But as a business owner, these became legitimate business expenses, reducing my taxable income."

Common deductible expenses for hobby-turned-businesses include:

1. Equipment and supplies
2. Home office space
3. Professional development

4. Marketing and advertising
5. Travel and vehicle expenses
6. Insurance and professional fees

The Home Office Advantage

Sarah Chen explains how the home office deduction can provide significant tax benefits: "Many retirees don't realize that using part of their home exclusively for business can create valuable tax deductions."

Michael Thompson's woodworking business provides a clear example. "I converted my garage into a dedicated workshop," he explains. "Because this space is used exclusively for my business, I can deduct a portion of our home's expenses, including utilities, insurance, and repairs."

Creating Tax-Efficient Income

Linda Peterson found that her gardening hobby could generate tax-efficient income through careful planning. "I started selling plants and offering garden design services," she shares. "But the real benefit came from understanding how to structure my income and expenses to maximize tax advantages."

Working with her tax advisor, Linda developed a strategy that included:

- Timing large equipment purchases for maximum tax benefit
- Hiring her grandchildren part-time during busy seasons
- Setting up a self-employed retirement plan
- Coordinating business income with other retirement income sources

"The key," Linda explains, "is understanding how your business income affects your overall tax situation. Sometimes, timing your income and expenses strategically can make a big difference in your tax bill."

Avoiding Common Pitfalls

Not every hobby-to-business transition succeeds. Sarah Chen shares some common mistakes she's seen:

"One retiree client tried to deduct all his golf expenses by claiming he was a golf consultant," she recalls. "But he couldn't demonstrate genuine efforts to make a profit. The IRS disallowed his deductions and assessed penalties."

The most successful transitions she's seen share common elements:

- Genuine effort to operate profitably
- Professional approach to operations
- Careful documentation of all activities
- Clear separation of business and personal expenses
- Regular consultation with tax professionals

NOTE: The **exclusive-use rule** requires that the home office space be used solely and regularly for business purposes. This deduction is only available to self-employed individuals or those running a legitimate business, not W-2 employees.

Acceptable Use: A spare bedroom used exclusively as a workspace for managing a woodworking business.

Unacceptable Use: A dining room used for business during the day and family meals at night.

Building for the Future

Patricia Harrison's art business has now grown beyond her initial expectations. "What started as a way to deduct my art expenses has become a fulfilling second career," she beams. "Last year, I made a genuine profit, and the tax benefits have been just one part of the reward."

The Thompsons, Petersons, and Harrisons all emphasize the importance of viewing their businesses as long-term ventures. "This isn't about creating artificial tax deductions,"

Michael Thompson explains. "It's about building something meaningful that also happens to have tax advantages."

Growing Your Business Strategically

Michael Thompson's woodworking business faced a turning point in its third year. "I had more orders than I could handle working alone," he explains from his expanded workshop, now twice its original size. "But I needed to think carefully about how growth would affect both our tax situation and our retirement lifestyle."

Working with his tax advisor, Michael explored several growth options:

- Hiring part-time help
- Expanding his workspace
- Automating certain processes
- Focusing on higher-margin custom pieces

"What we realized," Sarah Chen explains, working with clients like Michael, "is that business growth needs to align with your overall retirement and tax strategy. Sometimes, bigger isn't better from a tax perspective."

Balancing Business and Retirement

Patricia Harrison discovered that success brought its own challenges. "As my art business grew, I had to be careful not to let it take over my retirement," she shares. "The key was finding the sweet spot where the business provided tax benefits without becoming overwhelming."

She worked with her advisors to create what she calls her "three-part harmony":

1. Maintaining steady income from her FIA and other retirement sources
2. Managing her art business income to optimize tax benefits
3. Preserving time for family and personal activities

"The business should support your retirement lifestyle, not dominate it," Sarah Chen advises. "Many of my most successful clients are those who find this balance."

Leveraging Technology for Success

James Peterson found that technology could help him manage his photography business more efficiently while maintaining proper documentation for tax purposes. "I invested in software that tracks everything from mileage to inventory," he explains. "This not only saves time but also provides the detailed records the IRS likes to see."

Popular tools among successful hobby-turned-business owners include:

- Accounting software for accurate financial records
- Customer relationship management systems
- Inventory tracking applications
- Mileage and expense logging apps
- Digital receipt management

Creating a Legacy

For some retirees, their hobby-turned-business becomes more than just a tax strategy – it becomes a legacy to pass on to future generations. Linda Peterson's gardening business has become a family affair, with her daughter learning the business aspects while sharing her mother's passion for plants.

"We're now thinking about succession planning," Linda explains. "Having a legitimate business creates opportunities for tax-efficient wealth transfer that wouldn't exist if this were just a hobby."

Sarah Chen notes that business succession planning can offer significant tax advantages: "When structured properly, transitioning a business to the next generation can provide both income tax and estate tax benefits."

Adapting to Change

The most successful hobby-turned-business owners remain flexible and adaptable. Michael Thompson's woodworking business evolved when he discovered a niche market for custom furniture restoration. "Being adaptable not only helped the business grow but also created new tax planning opportunities," he shares.

Patricia Harrison faced similar evolution in her art business: "I started with local art fairs, but now I sell primarily through galleries and online. Each change required adjusting our tax strategy, but also opened new opportunities for deductions and income planning."

The Power of Community

One unexpected benefit many retirees discover is the community that develops around their business. "My workshop has become a gathering place for other woodworking enthusiasts," Michael explains. "Some have become customers, others have become suppliers, and many have become friends."

This community aspect can also create tax-advantaged opportunities:

- Joint marketing efforts with reduced costs

- Shared workspace arrangements
- Bulk purchasing discounts
- Knowledge sharing that reduces expensive mistakes
- Referral networks that lower marketing expenses

Bringing It All Together: The Art of Business in Retirement

As we conclude our exploration of turning hobbies into tax-advantaged businesses, let's return to Patricia Harrison's art studio one final time. "When I started this journey," she reflects, brushing final touches on her latest painting, "I thought I was just finding a way to deduct my art expenses. What I discovered was a whole new dimension to retirement."

The stories we've shared – from Michael's woodworking enterprise to Linda's gardening business and James's photography venture – illustrate that successful hobby-to-business transitions require a careful balance of passion and pragmatism. Each of these retirees found ways to transform their interests into legitimate businesses while creating valuable tax advantages.

"The key," Sarah Chen reminds us, "is remembering that this isn't about creating artificial deductions. It's about building something real that happens to have tax benefits as a natural result of proper business operation."

Michael Thompson offers a final perspective from his workshop, where he now mentors other retirees considering similar transitions: "This strategy works best when you approach it as a long-term commitment. The tax benefits are important, but they should flow from genuine business activity, not drive it."

Looking Ahead

As we move into our next chapter on Health Savings Accounts (HSAs), we'll explore another powerful tool for tax-efficient retirement planning. Linda Peterson, who now uses her gardening business income to fund her HSA, provides a perfect transition: "Understanding how different tax strategies can work together has been crucial. Our business income, combined with smart HSA planning, has given us more control over our retirement tax situation than we ever thought possible."

Remember these key points as we proceed:

- A hobby-to-business transition requires genuine profit motive and professional operation
- Proper documentation and business practices are essential for tax benefits
- Growth should align with your overall retirement goals
- Professional guidance helps optimize both business and tax outcomes

- The most successful transitions create value beyond tax advantages

Turn the page to discover how Health Savings Accounts can add another layer to your tax-efficient retirement strategy, potentially working alongside your business venture and other approaches we've discussed to create a more comprehensive approach to retirement tax planning.

References
Publication 535: Business Expenses

https://www.irs.gov/forms-pubs/about-publication-535

Publication 334: Tax Guide for Small Business

https://www.irs.gov/forms-pubs/about-publication-334

Publication 587: Business Use of Your Home

https://www.irs.gov/forms-pubs/about-publication-587

Jeff Weidner

CHAPTER 4: LEVERAGE HEALTH SAVINGS ACCOUNTS

The Triple Tax Advantage in Retirement Planning

Linda Peterson sat at her kitchen table, surrounded by medical bills and tax documents, when she first realized the full power of her Health Savings Account. "I had been contributing to my HSA for years," she explains, "but I hadn't grasped how it could transform our retirement tax strategy until I saw the numbers in black and white."

Like many retirees, Linda and James Peterson initially viewed their HSA simply as a way to handle current medical expenses. Their perspective changed dramatically when their financial advisor showed them how an HSA could serve as a powerful tax planning tool for retirement.

The Thompson's HSA Discovery

Michael and Sarah Thompson, whom we've followed through previous chapters, made a similar discovery. "We were focused on Michael's woodworking business and our Fixed Indexed Annuity strategy," Sarah recalls, "when our tax advisor pointed out we weren't maximizing one of the best tax advantages available to us – our Health Savings Account."

The Thompsons learned that HSAs offer a unique triple tax advantage:

1. Tax-deductible contributions
2. Tax-free growth
3. Tax-free withdrawals for qualified medical expenses

NOTE: For the 2025 tax year, Health Savings Account (HSA) contribution limits are as follows:

Self-Only Coverage: Up to $4,300.

Family Coverage: Up to $8,550.

Catch-Up Contribution: Individuals aged 55 or older can contribute an additional $1,000.

To be eligible to contribute to an HSA, you must be enrolled in a High Deductible Health Plan (HDHP). For 2025, an HDHP is defined as a plan with:

Minimum Annual Deductible: $1,650 for self-only coverage; $3,300 for family coverage.

Maximum Annual Out-of-Pocket Expenses: $8,300 for self-only coverage; $16,600 for family coverage.

These limits are set by the IRS and are subject to annual adjustments.

Early, non-qualified withdrawals from an HSA are subject to a 20% penalty and income tax if taken before age 65. After

65, non-qualified withdrawals are taxed as income but avoid the penalty. Qualified expenses include prescription medications, dental care, vision care, and Medicare premiums. Always verify expenses with IRS guidelines.

"What really caught our attention," Michael adds, leaning forward in his chair, "was learning that there's no time limit on when we need to reimburse ourselves for medical expenses. This opened up some interesting planning opportunities we hadn't considered."

The Williams' Strategic Approach

Mark and Jennifer Williams, both 58, provide an excellent example of strategic HSA planning. When we meet them in their modest suburban home, they're eager to share how they transformed their approach to healthcare saving.

"We had a wake-up call," Jennifer explains, pulling out a folder of carefully organized medical receipts. "Fidelity had just released their latest estimate that a retired couple our age would need around $315,000 for healthcare costs in retirement. That number got our attention."

Working with their financial advisor, the Williams developed a comprehensive HSA strategy:

1. Maximized annual HSA contributions
2. Paid current medical expenses from other sources

3. Invested their HSA funds for long-term growth
4. Kept meticulous records of all medical expenses
5. Planned for future Medicare premium payments

"The key insight," Mark shares, "was understanding that we could let our HSA grow tax-free while paying medical expenses out of pocket. We save all our medical receipts, knowing we can reimburse ourselves tax-free at any point in the future."

NOTE: Some HSA providers offer only savings accounts and that readers should confirm investment options when selecting an HSA provider. Include a disclaimer about the risks of investing HSA funds and the importance of maintaining a balance for near-term medical expenses.

Understanding the Numbers

Sarah Chen, our tax advisor from previous chapters, explains how the Williams' strategy works in practice: "In 2024, they can contribute $8,300 to their family HSA, plus an additional $1,000 catch-up contribution since they're over 55. That's $9,300 in tax-deductible contributions each year."

The Williams' five-year results demonstrate the power of this approach:

- Accumulated $85,000 in their HSA
- Documented $32,000 in out-of-pocket medical expenses

- Created flexible tax-free withdrawal options for the future
- Generated tax savings of approximately $28,000
- Established a growing healthcare fund for retirement

The Investment Strategy Revelation

Jennifer Williams remembers the moment their perspective on HSAs shifted completely. "We were having coffee with Linda Peterson, talking about her gardening business, when she mentioned that she invests her HSA funds just like her IRA," Jennifer recalls. "Until then, we'd kept our HSA in a savings account, not realizing its growth potential."

This conversation led the Williams to explore investment options within their HSA. Working with their advisor, they developed an investment strategy that aligned with their long-term goals. "We learned that since we were paying current medical expenses out of pocket, we could invest our HSA more aggressively," Mark explains. "It's money we don't need to touch for years, potentially decades."

Their HSA investment strategy focused on:

- Long-term growth potential
- Diversification across asset classes
- Regular rebalancing
- Low-cost investment options
- Tax-efficient fund choices

The Medicare Premium Solution

The Petersons discovered another valuable use for their HSA when they reached Medicare age. "What many people don't realize," James Peterson explains, "is that you can use HSA funds tax-free to pay Medicare premiums. This was a game-changer for our retirement budget planning."

Linda adds an important detail: "We had accumulated significant HSA funds before enrolling in Medicare. Now we use these tax-free dollars to cover our Part B and D premiums, which helps manage our overall retirement tax situation."

Sarah Chen elaborates on this strategy: "Medicare premiums can be a significant retirement expense. Being able to pay them with tax-free HSA dollars effectively reduces the after-tax cost of healthcare in retirement."

Family Coordination Strategies

The Thompson family found ways to maximize their HSA benefits through careful family planning. "When our daughter started her own business," Sarah Thompson shares, "we helped her understand how to coordinate her

HSA with her self-employed health insurance. It became a family discussion about long-term tax planning."

Michael notes how this fits into their larger family financial strategy: "We realized that helping our children maximize their HSAs early in their careers could significantly impact their long-term financial health. It's become part of our family's financial education tradition."

Documentation: The Key to Success

Mark Williams' background in accounting made him particularly attuned to the importance of documentation. In his home office, he demonstrates his organization system: "I created a digital filing system for all our medical receipts. Each expense is categorized, dated, and stored both digitally and in hard copy."

Their system includes:

- Digital scans of all medical receipts
- A spreadsheet tracking expenses and reimbursements
- Annual summaries of qualified medical expenses
- Backup copies stored securely in the cloud
- Regular reconciliation with HSA statements

"The peace of mind this organization provides is invaluable," Jennifer adds. "We know exactly how much we can withdraw tax-free at any time, whether next year or twenty years from now."

Planning for the Unexpected

The Williams' careful planning proved particularly valuable when Mark faced an unexpected health challenge. "Last year, I needed surgery that wasn't entirely covered by our insurance," he explains. "Having a well-funded HSA meant we could handle the expenses without disrupting our other retirement plans."

Their experience highlights several key aspects of HSA planning:

- The importance of maintaining an emergency medical fund
- The flexibility to handle unexpected healthcare costs
- The value of long-term tax free growth
- The peace of mind that comes with proper planning
- The ability to adapt to changing health needs

Integration with Other Retirement Strategies

Linda Peterson's gardening business provides an excellent example of how HSAs can work alongside other retirement tax strategies. "When I started generating income from my business," she explains, working at her potting bench, "I realized I could use some of that revenue to maximize our HSA contributions while still qualifying for tax deductions through the business."

The Petersons worked with their tax advisor to create a comprehensive strategy that coordinated their various tax advantages:

- HSA contributions from business income
- Business expense deductions
- Strategic timing of medical expenses
- Coordination with their Fixed Indexed Annuity income
- Integration with their overall retirement withdrawal strategy

The State Tax Consideration

The Williams discovered another layer of HSA benefits when researching state tax implications. "We learned that most states that have an income tax follow the federal tax treatment of HSAs," Mark explains, surrounded by tax planning documents. "This meant we were getting triple tax advantages at both the federal and state levels."

Sarah Chen notes that this state tax benefit can be significant: "For clients in high-tax states, the state tax savings alone can make HSA contributions worthwhile. It's like getting an extra bonus on top of the federal tax benefits."

Common Mistakes and How to Avoid Them

Through her years of advising retirees, Sarah Chen has observed several common HSA mistakes. She shares these through the experiences of her clients who learned valuable lessons:

"One couple I work with initially made the mistake of using their HSA funds for every minor medical expense," she recalls. "They didn't realize they were giving up years of potential tax-free growth. Now they understand the value of letting their HSA grow while paying smaller expenses out of pocket."

Michael Thompson admits to almost making a similar mistake: "When we first started with our HSA, I thought we had to use it or lose it, like a Flexible Spending Account. Learning the difference completely changed our approach to healthcare saving."

The Next Generation Approach

The Thompson's daughter, Emily, represents a younger generation taking HSA lessons from their parents' experience. "Watching my parents use their HSA strategically inspired me to start maximizing my own contributions early," she shares during a family gathering. "I'm treating it like a specialized retirement account that can help me manage healthcare costs throughout my life."

Her approach demonstrates how HSA strategies can evolve across generations:

- Starting contributions early in her career
- Investing aggressively for long-term growth
- Maintaining detailed records from the beginning
- Coordinating with other retirement savings
- Planning for future healthcare needs

Looking to the Future

As healthcare costs continue to rise, the Williams see their HSA strategy as increasingly important. "We view our HSA as a crucial part of our retirement planning," Jennifer explains. "It's not just about managing current medical expenses – it's about having tax-efficient funds available for healthcare throughout our retirement."

Mark adds a practical perspective: "The ability to pay Medicare premiums and other healthcare costs with tax-free dollars gives us more flexibility in managing our other retirement income sources. It's all interconnected."

Bringing It All Together: The Strategic Power of HSAs

Sitting in their garden, surrounded by the fruits of Linda's business labor, the Petersons reflect on their HSA journey. "What started as a simple healthcare savings account has become a cornerstone of our retirement tax strategy," Linda shares, gesturing toward her meticulously maintained receipt files. "It's amazing how something that seems so straightforward can have such far-reaching benefits."

The experiences we've shared – from the Williams' sophisticated investment approach to the Thompsons' family legacy planning and Emily's next-generation implementation – demonstrate the versatility and power of Health Savings Accounts in retirement planning. Each family found ways to maximize the triple tax advantage while integrating their HSA strategy with their broader retirement plans.

"The key," Sarah Chen reminds us, "is thinking of your HSA as more than just a healthcare fund. It's a powerful tax planning tool that can provide flexibility and security throughout retirement."

Mark Williams offers a final perspective from his home office, where his digital filing system has become a model for other retirees: "Success with HSAs comes from understanding both the rules and the opportunities. The tax benefits are substantial, but they require careful planning and documentation to maximize their value."

Looking Ahead

As we move into our next chapter on Opportunity Zones, we'll explore another powerful strategy for tax-efficient investing in retirement. Jennifer Williams, who has begun exploring Opportunity Zone investments with some of their HSA gains, provides a perfect transition: "We've learned that successful retirement tax planning often involves combining multiple strategies. Understanding how Opportunity Zones can work alongside our HSA and other retirement accounts has opened up new possibilities for tax-efficient wealth building."

Remember these key points as we proceed:

- HSAs offer unique triple tax advantages that few other accounts provide
- Strategic use of HSAs can significantly impact your retirement tax situation
- Proper documentation is crucial for long-term success

- Integration with other retirement strategies maximizes benefits
- Early planning and consistent execution yield the best results

Turn the page to discover how Opportunity Zones can add another dimension to your tax-efficient retirement strategy, potentially working in concert with your HSA and other approaches we've discussed to create an even more robust approach to retirement tax planning. As we'll see, the careful documentation habits you've developed with your HSA will serve you well in navigating the opportunities and requirements of Opportunity Zone investments.

References

Publication 969: Health Savings Accounts and Other Tax-Favored Health Plans

https://www.irs.gov/forms-pubs/about-publication-969

Publication 502: Medical and Dental Expenses **https://www.irs.gov/forms-pubs/about-publication-502**

CHAPTER 5: INVEST IN OPPORTUNITY ZONES

Strategic Tax-Advantaged Real Estate Investment in Retirement

Jennifer Williams never expected to become an expert in Opportunity Zone investments. Standing at the window of her recently renovated office building in a developing neighborhood, she reflects on the journey that began with a simple question: "What should we do with the proceeds from selling our family business?"

That question led the Williams family to discover one of the most powerful tax advantages created by the Tax Cuts and Jobs Act of 2017 - Opportunity Zones. Their story, along with others we'll meet in this chapter, illustrates how retirees can use these special investment zones to defer capital gains while supporting community development.

Understanding the Opportunity

Mark Williams leans back in his chair in their new office, surrounded by maps and development plans. "When our advisor first mentioned Opportunity Zones, I was skeptical," he admits. "It sounded too good to be true - defer capital gains taxes while investing in real estate development? But the more we learned, the more we realized this could be a perfect fit for our retirement strategy."

The Williams had just sold their family business for $2.8 million, generating significant capital gains. Their financial advisor, Sarah Chen, recognized an opportunity to help them defer taxes while creating a new stream of retirement income.

"Opportunity Zones offer three distinct tax benefits," Sarah explains, pointing to a diagram on her tablet:

1. Temporary deferral of capital gains taxes
2. Partial reduction of the deferred gain
3. Permanent exclusion of gains on the Opportunity Zone investment if held for 10 years

The Harrison's Discovery

Robert and Patricia Harrison, whom we met earlier discussing their art business and HSA strategy, found their way into Opportunity Zone investing through a different path. "We had inherited a property in California that had appreciated significantly," Patricia explains. "Selling it would have triggered a large capital gains tax bill. That's when our advisor suggested we look into Opportunity Zones."

The Harrisons worked with their tax and legal team to structure their investment carefully:

1. Sold the inherited property
2. Identified a suitable Opportunity Zone project
3. Invested through a Qualified Opportunity Fund
4. Developed a long-term holding strategy

"What appealed to us most," Robert shares, "was the ability to transform a taxable event into an investment that could generate income throughout our retirement while supporting community development."

The Mechanics of Opportunity Zone Investing

Sarah Chen explains the importance of understanding the technical requirements through the Williams' experience: "Jennifer and Mark had 180 days from selling their business to invest in a Qualified Opportunity Fund. Timing is crucial with these investments."

Making the Investment Work

Jennifer Williams walks through the renovated building that now houses several thriving small businesses. "We didn't just want to invest money," she explains, "we wanted to create something meaningful for our retirement years while taking advantage of the tax benefits."

The Williams' approach to their Opportunity Zone investment involved careful consideration of several factors:

Mark pulls out their original planning documents: "We learned that success in Opportunity Zone investing requires more than just finding a qualifying location. You need to understand the community, the market potential, and most importantly, the strict compliance requirements."

Their project evolved through several stages:

First Year:

"We spent months researching different Opportunity Zones," Jennifer recalls. "Some looked good on paper but didn't have the growth potential we were seeking. We finally found this building in an area where other development was already starting to happen."

Second Year:

"The renovation phase was crucial," Mark adds. "The rules require you to substantially improve the property - basically doubling your initial investment in the building itself. We worked with local contractors and architects to create something the community needed."

Third Year:

"That's when we started seeing real results," Jennifer smiles. "New tenants moved in, other developers began projects nearby, and we could see our vision coming to life."

The Partnership Approach

The Harrisons took a different route, choosing to invest through a professionally managed Qualified Opportunity Fund rather than directly managing a property. "We wanted the tax benefits without becoming developers ourselves," Patricia explains from their home office, where she continues to run her art business.

Robert elaborates on their decision: "We invested in a fund that focuses on multi-family housing development. It gave us exposure to Opportunity Zone benefits while leaving the complex compliance requirements to professional managers."

Their fund investment provided several advantages:

- Professional management of all compliance requirements
- Diversification across multiple properties
- Regular income distributions
- Reduced personal involvement
- Simplified tax reporting

Understanding the Risks

Sarah Chen emphasizes the importance of recognizing both the opportunities and challenges of Opportunity Zone investments. "These aren't get-rich-quick investments," she cautions. "They require patient capital and careful attention to compliance requirements."

She shares a story of another client who learned this lesson the hard way: "They rushed into an Opportunity Zone investment without proper due diligence. Six months in, they discovered their property didn't qualify for the program because they hadn't structured the purchase correctly. It's crucial to work with advisors who understand these complex rules."

The Community Impact

For the Williams, their Opportunity Zone investment has become more than just a tax strategy. Jennifer gestures toward the street where new businesses have opened: "We've watched this neighborhood transform. What started as a tax-advantaged investment has become a legacy project that benefits both our retirement plan and the community."

Mark adds a practical perspective: "The tax benefits attracted us initially, but the real satisfaction comes from seeing how our investment has helped create jobs and revitalize the area. Plus, the property's value has increased significantly, which will be tax-free if we hold it for the full 10-year period."

Long-Term Planning Considerations

The Peterson family's experience adds another dimension to our understanding of Opportunity Zone investing. James Peterson, who we previously met discussing his photography business and HSA strategy, discovered an unexpected synergy between his various retirement ventures.

"We realized we could use income from our Opportunity Zone investment to fund our HSA and other retirement accounts," James explains, reviewing his financial planning documents. "It's all about creating an integrated strategy where each piece complements the others."

Linda Peterson adds insight from their experience: "The key is thinking beyond the initial tax deferral. We're building a legacy that can benefit our children and grandchildren while supporting community development."

Their long-term strategy incorporates several elements:

- Regular income generation from tenant leases
- Property appreciation potential
- Future development opportunities
- Family succession planning
- Community involvement

The Technical Requirements

Sarah Chen emphasizes the importance of understanding the technical aspects of Opportunity Zone investments through the experiences of her clients. "The Williams' success wasn't just about choosing the right property," she explains. "It was about following the rules meticulously."

Key compliance requirements include:

1. Investment Timing

"You must invest capital gains within 180 days of realizing them," Mark Williams explains. "We actually had to accelerate the sale of our business to meet the investment window for a particular property we had identified."

2. Substantial Improvement

"This was a big one," Jennifer adds. "We had to document how we would invest at least as much in improvements as we paid for the building itself, excluding the land value."

3. Holding Period

"The tax benefits increase the longer you hold the investment," Robert Harrison notes. "We structured our fund investment with a clear 10-year horizon to maximize the benefits."

Managing Multiple Investments

The Williams' success with their first Opportunity Zone project led them to consider additional investments. Jennifer shares their thought process: "After seeing the positive results from our first project, we identified another opportunity in a neighboring zone. But we knew we needed to approach it differently."

Their second investment involved:

- Partnership with experienced developers
- Focus on a different property type
- New financing strategies
- Enhanced community engagement
- Different tenant mix

"Each project teaches you something new," Mark reflects. "Our second investment benefited from everything we learned in the first one, but it also presented its own unique challenges and opportunities."

The Future of Opportunity Zones

The evolution of Opportunity Zone investments continues to create new possibilities for retirees. Sarah Chen shares her perspective on emerging trends:

"We're seeing more creative approaches to Opportunity Zone investing," she explains. "Some clients are combining these investments with other tax strategies, like using Qualified Opportunity Funds in conjunction with charitable giving or estate planning."

The Harrisons recently explored such a combination strategy. "We're looking at ways to eventually transition our fund investment to our children," Patricia explains, "while maintaining the tax benefits and continuing the positive community impact."

Building Lasting Value: The Promise of Opportunity Zones

Standing in front of their renovated building at sunset, Jennifer and Mark Williams reflect on their journey into Opportunity Zone investing. "What began as a tax strategy has become something much more meaningful," Jennifer says, watching evening customers stream into the new café on the ground floor. "We've created lasting value – for our retirement, for our family, and for this community."

The stories we've shared – from the Williams' direct property development to the Harrisons' fund investment approach and the Petersons' integrated strategy – demonstrate the versatility of Opportunity Zone investments. Each family found ways to align these tax advantages with their broader retirement goals while contributing to community development.

"The key," Sarah Chen reminds us, "is understanding that Opportunity Zone investments are long-term commitments. The tax benefits are significant, but they should support, not drive, your investment decisions."

Robert Harrison offers a final perspective from his experience with fund investing: "Success with Opportunity

Zones requires careful planning, patient capital, and a clear vision for what you want to achieve. The tax benefits are important, but the real reward comes from creating something of lasting value."

Looking Ahead

As we move into our next chapter on claiming tax benefits while supporting family members, we'll explore how to extend your tax-efficient retirement strategy to benefit those closest to you. The Williams' daughter, Amy, provides a perfect transition: "Watching my parents develop their Opportunity Zone project inspired me to think differently about combining business success with family support. Now, as they help me with my children's education expenses, we're discovering new ways to create tax advantages that benefit multiple generations."

Remember these key points as we proceed:

- Opportunity Zones offer powerful tax benefits for patient investors
- Success requires careful attention to technical requirements
- Professional guidance is essential for compliance
- Community impact can enhance investment returns
- Long-term planning creates multi-generational benefits

Turn the page to discover how supporting your family members can create additional tax advantages, potentially working alongside your Opportunity Zone investments and other strategies we've discussed. As we'll see, the patient, long-term approach you've developed with Opportunity Zone investing can also enhance your family tax planning strategies.

After all, as Jennifer Williams notes while locking up her office for the evening, "Everything we do in retirement planning is ultimately about family – creating security for ourselves while building opportunities for the next generation."

References

Publication 544: Sales and Other Dispositions of Assets

https://www.irs.gov/forms-pubs/about-publication-554

Notice 2021: Relief for Qualified Opportunity Funds

https://www.irs.gov/retirement-plans/retirement-plans-notices

CHAPTER 6: CLAIM THE TAX BENEFITS OF SUPPORTING YOUR FAMILY

Maximizing Tax Advantages While Supporting Loved Ones

Amy Williams never expected her parents' retirement tax planning would benefit her young family so directly. Sitting at her kitchen table, surrounded by her children's school documents and medical bills, she shares how her parents' strategic approach to family support has created tax advantages for multiple generations.

"When Mom and Jennifer first explained how they were structuring their family support to maximize tax benefits, I was skeptical," Amy admits, sorting through carefully organized receipts. "But now I see how their planning has helped both their retirement strategy and our family's financial security."

The Multi-Generation Approach

Jennifer and Mark Williams had always planned to help their children and grandchildren financially. However, their experience with Opportunity Zone investing taught them the value of strategic tax planning. Working with Sarah Chen, they developed a comprehensive approach to family support that maximized tax benefits while helping their loved ones.

"The key was understanding how different types of support are treated for tax purposes," Sarah explains from her office, pulling up the Williams family file. "Some forms of family support offer immediate tax benefits, while others create long-term advantages for both the givers and recipients."

The Martinez Family Strategy

Let's meet Richard and Elena Martinez, who have developed their own approach to tax-efficient family support. At 67, they found themselves helping their daughter through graduate school while also supporting Elena's elderly mother.

"We needed to balance multiple responsibilities," Elena explains from their home office, where she tracks family expenses. "We wanted to help both the younger and older generations while managing our own retirement tax situation."

Working with their advisors, the Martinez family created a structured support system:

- Direct tuition payments for their daughter's education
- Coordinated medical expense payments for Elena's mother
- Strategic gifting programs for their grandchildren
- Documented dependent care arrangements
- Integrated support with their retirement distributions

"What surprised us," Richard shares, "was how many tax benefits were available when we structured our family support properly. We just needed to understand the rules and maintain careful documentation."

Education Support: Beyond Basic Tuition

Elena Martinez pulls out a spreadsheet detailing her daughter's graduate school expenses. "We discovered that direct tuition payments to educational institutions offered unique tax advantages," she explains. "These payments didn't count against our annual gift tax exclusion, allowing us to provide additional support in other ways."

The Martinez family worked with Sarah Chen to implement a comprehensive education support strategy:

"The first step," Sarah explains, "was understanding the difference between direct tuition payments and other educational support. The tax implications vary significantly depending on how you structure the assistance."

Richard adds practical insight from their experience: "We pay tuition directly to the university, which doesn't count toward gift tax limits. Then we use our annual gift exclusion to help with books, housing, and other expenses. This maximizes the tax benefits while providing comprehensive support."

Healthcare Support Strategies

The Williams family found creative ways to combine healthcare support with tax advantages. Amy gestures toward a filing cabinet containing medical records: "Mom and Dad helped us set up our own HSA and taught us how to coordinate medical expenses across generations."

Their approach includes:

- Direct payments to medical providers
- Coordination with family HSA accounts
- Documentation of qualified medical expenses
- Strategic timing of support payments
- Integration with their own retirement healthcare planning

Jennifer Williams explains their thinking: "We learned from our own HSA experience that healthcare planning needs to be multi-generational. By helping our children establish their own HSAs while we make direct medical payments when needed, we're creating tax advantages that benefit everyone."

The Dependent Care Advantage

The Martinez family's support of Elena's mother illustrates another aspect of tax-efficient family support. "When Mom needed more care, we discovered various tax benefits associated with dependent care," Elena explains, showing a carefully organized care calendar.

Their strategy involved:

1. Documenting qualifying dependent status
2. Tracking care expenses
3. Coordinating caregiver payments
4. Managing household support costs
5. Integrating medical expenses

"What many people don't realize," Sarah Chen notes, "is that dependent care tax benefits can apply to both children and elderly parents. The key is understanding the qualification requirements and maintaining proper documentation."

Strategic Gifting Programs

The Williams family developed a systematic approach to gifting that maximizes tax benefits while supporting their family's needs. "We learned that timing and structure matter significantly when it comes to gifts," Mark explains, reviewing their family gifting calendar.

Jennifer adds insight from their experience: "By coordinating our gifting strategy with other family support, we've been able to help more while keeping everything tax-efficient."

Their gifting program includes several key elements:

Annual Gift Planning:
"We use a calendar to track all gifts," Jennifer explains, showing a detailed spreadsheet. "This ensures we maximize annual exclusions without exceeding limits. For 2024, that means we can each give up to $17,000 to each family member without gift tax implications."

Educational Support:
Mark points to their grandchildren's college planning documents: "Direct tuition payments don't count against gift tax limits, so we coordinate these with our regular gifting

program. This allows us to provide more substantial support while maintaining tax efficiency."

Medical Expense Coordination:
"Similar to education expenses," Jennifer notes, "direct payments to medical providers don't count toward gift limits. We've used this to help with everything from unexpected medical bills to ongoing healthcare needs."

Real Estate Strategies

The Martinez family found creative ways to use real estate in their family support strategy. Elena shares their approach from the in-law suite they added to their home: "When Mom needed more care, we explored how to use our home to provide support while maximizing tax benefits."

Their strategy involved several components:

Home Modifications:
"We documented all the modifications required for Mom's care," Richard explains. "Many of these qualified as medical expenses, providing tax benefits while creating a better living situation."

Space Allocation:

Elena points out various features of their modified home: "By properly documenting the space used exclusively for Mom's care, we were able to optimize our tax deductions while providing the support she needed."

Business Integration

The Williams found ways to integrate family support with their business ventures. Amy now manages part of their Opportunity Zone property, creating employment opportunities while maintaining tax efficiency.

"It's about finding win-win situations," Mark explains. "By employing family members in legitimate business roles, we can provide support while creating tax-advantaged income for them."

Sarah Chen emphasizes the importance of proper documentation: "Family employment must be legitimate and well-documented. The work must be necessary, the compensation reasonable, and all employment requirements met."

Coordinating Multiple Support Strategies

The complexity of managing various family support methods became clear when the Martinez family faced multiple needs simultaneously. Elena pulls out a timeline she created to track different support activities: "We had Mom's medical needs, our daughter's graduate school, and our grandchildren's education all happening at once. Coordination became crucial."

Richard explains their solution: "We created what we call our 'Family Support Calendar' that helps us track and coordinate different types of assistance throughout the year."

Their coordinated approach includes:

Quarterly Planning:
"We review all upcoming needs every three months," Elena explains. "This helps us time our support for maximum tax efficiency."

Documentation Systems:
Richard demonstrates their digital filing system: "Every expense, every gift, every payment is categorized and documented. This makes tax time much easier and helps us stay compliant."

Professional Coordination:
"We meet with our tax advisor regularly," Elena adds. "These meetings help us adjust our strategy as family needs and tax laws change."

Special Situations and Solutions

The Williams family encountered several unique situations that required creative problem-solving. Amy shares an experience from when her children needed special educational support: "Mom and Dad helped us navigate the tax implications of various therapy and educational services, finding ways to maximize deductions while getting the kids the help they needed."

Their approach to special situations involved:

Research and Documentation:
"We learned to research thoroughly before making decisions," Jennifer explains. "Some expenses that seemed purely educational actually qualified as medical expenses, changing how we structured the support."

Professional Guidance:
Mark emphasizes the importance of expert help: "When situations get complex, having professional guidance becomes crucial. Our tax advisor helped us understand options we hadn't considered."

Flexible Implementation:
"We learned to build flexibility into our plans," Amy notes. "Family needs change, and our support strategies needed to adapt while maintaining tax efficiency."

Creating Teaching Moments

Both families discovered that their strategic approach to family support created valuable teaching opportunities. "We're not just providing financial help," Elena explains, "we're teaching the next generation about tax-efficient financial management."

Their educational approach includes:

Regular Family Meetings:
"We hold quarterly family financial discussions," Richard shares. "Everyone learns about tax strategy, documentation requirements, and long-term planning."

Practical Application:
"We involve our children in the planning process," Jennifer adds. "They learn by participating in real decisions about family support."

Building Long-Term Family Financial Literacy

Amy Williams has started implementing lessons learned from her parents in her own family's financial planning. Sitting at her kitchen table after one of their quarterly family meetings, she shares how these discussions have evolved: "What started as conversations about tax-efficient support has become a comprehensive family financial education program."

Her children, now teenagers, participate in age-appropriate ways. "Even my fourteen-year-old understands the basics of tax-advantaged gifting," she says proudly. "These aren't just abstract concepts to them anymore."

The Williams' approach to family financial education includes:

Practical Learning Experiences:
"When we help with college savings," Jennifer explains, "we show the grandchildren how 529 plans work, why we choose certain investment options, and how tax benefits affect long-term growth."

Documentation Practice:
Mark demonstrates their system: "We teach the kids to keep records of their own expenses and earnings. They're learning habits that will serve them well throughout their lives."

Adapting to Changing Family Needs

The Martinez family's experience demonstrates how support strategies must evolve with family circumstances. Elena shares their perspective from recent changes: "As Mom's needs increased and our daughter finished graduate school, we had to adjust our approach while maintaining tax efficiency."

Their adaptation strategy involves:

Regular Assessment:
"We review family needs monthly now," Richard explains. "This allows us to adjust support levels and methods as circumstances change."

Flexible Support Methods:

Elena points to their updated planning documents: "We've learned to maintain flexibility in how we provide support, always looking for the most tax-efficient options available."

Integrating with Estate Planning

Both families have discovered the importance of coordinating current support with long-term estate planning. Sarah Chen explains: "Tax-efficient family support during your lifetime can significantly impact your estate planning options."

The Williams' integrated approach includes:

Lifetime Gifting Strategies:
"We're essentially doing estate planning in real-time," Mark explains. "By using annual gifts and direct payments for education and medical expenses, we're reducing our taxable estate while helping family members when they need it most."

Future Planning:
Jennifer shares their perspective: "Every support decision we make considers both immediate tax benefits and long-term estate implications."

Creating a Legacy of Financial Wisdom

As the sun sets outside the Martinez family home, Elena and Richard sit in their carefully planned in-law suite, reflecting on their journey of family support. "What began as a search for tax-efficient ways to help our loved ones has become something much more meaningful," Elena shares, gesturing to the family photos that line the walls. "We've created not just financial support, but a legacy of financial wisdom."

The stories we've shared – from the Williams' comprehensive gifting strategy to the Martinez family's coordinated support approach – demonstrate how thoughtful planning can multiply the impact of family assistance. Each family found ways to maximize tax benefits while creating lasting value across generations.

"The real success," Sarah Chen observes, "isn't just in the tax savings, though those are significant. It's in teaching families how to think strategically about financial decisions and support."

Amy Williams offers a final perspective from her kitchen, where family financial discussions have become a regular part of life: "We're not just receiving support; we're learning and teaching our children how to manage resources wisely.

The tax benefits are important, but the knowledge transfer is invaluable."

Looking Ahead

As we move into our next chapter on tax-loss harvesting, we'll explore how to further optimize your investment strategy for tax efficiency. Mark Williams provides a perfect transition: "After mastering family support strategies, we realized we could apply similar strategic thinking to our investment portfolio. Tax-loss harvesting became another tool in our tax-efficiency toolkit, often providing resources for family support."

Remember these key points as we proceed:

- Family support can be structured for maximum tax efficiency
- Proper documentation is essential for all support strategies
- Coordination between different support methods enhances benefits
- Education and knowledge transfer create lasting value
- Integration with other tax strategies multiplies advantages

Turn the page to discover how tax-loss harvesting can add another dimension to your tax-efficient retirement strategy. As Jennifer Williams notes while reviewing their family's quarterly investment reports, "Every tax dollar saved through smart investment strategies is another dollar available for family support. It's all connected."

After all, as Richard Martinez reminds us, looking at three generations of his family gathered for their regular financial discussion, "The most valuable legacy we can leave isn't just financial support – it's the knowledge of how to manage and preserve wealth across generations."

References

Publication 503: Child and Dependent Care Expenses

Information

https://www.irs.gov/forms-pubs/about-publication-503

Publication 501: Dependents, Standard Deduction, and Filing

https://www.irs.gov/forms-pubs/about-publication-501

CHAPTER 7: HARVEST TAX LOSSES IN YOUR PORTFOLIO

Understanding and Implementing Tax-Loss Harvesting

Understanding Tax-Loss Harvesting: The Basics

Tax-loss harvesting might sound complicated, but at its heart, it's a straightforward concept that can save you significant money on taxes. Think of it as finding a silver lining in investment losses. When the value of an investment falls below what you paid for it, you can sell it and use that loss to reduce your taxes. The best part? You can reinvest the money right away to maintain your investment strategy, as long as you follow some specific rules.

Let's break this down with a simple example. Imagine you bought some shares of stock for $10,000, and their value has dropped to $7,000. By selling these shares, you create a $3,000 loss that you can use to offset other gains in your portfolio. If you don't have any gains to offset, you can use up to $3,000 of investment losses to reduce your regular income for the year. Any additional losses can be saved and used in future years.

How Tax-Loss Harvesting Works in Practice

The process of tax-loss harvesting requires careful attention to timing and investment selection. When you sell an investment at a loss, you'll want to reinvest that money right away to stay in the market. However, you need to be careful about what you buy. The IRS doesn't want people to simply sell and immediately repurchase the same investment just to create tax losses. They created what's called the "wash sale rule" to prevent this practice.

The wash sale rule says you can't buy the same investment, or one that is "substantially identical," within 30 days before or after selling at a loss. If you do, you can't claim the tax loss. This rule applies to all your accounts, including IRAs, so you need to keep track of your investments across everything you own.

Tax-loss harvesting can be a valuable strategy for retirees to offset capital gains and reduce taxable income, but it comes with important considerations. The wash sale rule disallows losses if the same or a substantially identical security is purchased within 30 days before or after the sale, so careful planning is essential. Additionally, net losses can offset only up to $3,000 of ordinary income annually, with the remainder carried forward to future years. Keep in mind that this strategy applies exclusively to taxable accounts, as retirement accounts like IRAs and 401(k)s do not generate taxable capital gains or losses.

Let's say you want to sell shares of a large-company stock fund to harvest a loss. Instead of buying back the same fund, you might purchase a different fund that invests in similar companies but tracks a different index. This way, you maintain your investment strategy while still qualifying for the tax loss.

The Long-Term Impact on Your Retirement

Tax-loss harvesting can be particularly valuable in retirement when managing your tax bracket becomes crucial. Every dollar of tax you save through careful loss harvesting is a dollar you can use for other purposes. Over time, these savings can add up to significant amounts that can help fund your retirement lifestyle or provide additional resources for family support.

Timing Your Tax-Loss Harvesting

Many people only think about tax-loss harvesting in December, when they're getting ready to file their taxes. However, the most successful retirement investors know that opportunities for tax-loss harvesting can appear throughout the year. Market volatility, while sometimes unsettling, can create chances to capture valuable tax losses while maintaining your long-term investment strategy.

Consider how Mark Williams approaches this in his retirement portfolio. "I used to panic when I saw investments decline in value," he explains from his home office. "Now I understand that market declines can create tax-saving opportunities if handled correctly." Mark reviews his investments monthly, looking for positions that have dropped below their purchase price. When he finds them, he considers whether harvesting the loss makes sense as part of his overall strategy.

Maintaining Your Investment Strategy

One of the biggest challenges in tax-loss harvesting is staying invested while following the wash sale rules. You don't want to sit in cash while waiting for the 30-day wash sale period to pass. This is where careful planning becomes essential. You need to have alternative investments ready that will keep your money working while satisfying IRS requirements.

Jennifer Williams learned this lesson through experience. "The first time we harvested losses, we were so focused on avoiding wash sales that we left the money in cash for several weeks," she recalls. "The market recovered during that time, and we missed out on potential gains. Now we have a plan for every investment we might need to sell."

Their solution was to create a list of alternative investments for each major position in their portfolio. When they need to sell something to capture a loss, they immediately know what to buy instead. This keeps their investment strategy on track while securing valuable tax benefits.

The Impact on Retirement Income

Tax-loss harvesting becomes even more valuable when coordinated with other retirement income strategies. Michael and Sarah Thompson discovered this when managing withdrawals from their various accounts. "We realized that by harvesting losses strategically, we could help control our taxable income," Michael explains. "This affected everything from our Medicare premiums to how much of our Social Security was taxed."

The Thompsons work with their financial advisor to look at their entire financial picture when making tax-loss harvesting decisions. They consider questions like: How will realizing this loss affect their tax bracket? Could the loss help offset gains from other necessary portfolio changes? How might this impact their required minimum distributions?

Making Tax-Loss Harvesting Work for Your Retirement

As the sun sets outside their home office window, Mark and Jennifer Williams review their latest tax-loss harvesting results. "What started as a way to make the best of market downturns has become an integral part of our retirement tax strategy," Jennifer reflects. "We've learned that success comes from consistent monitoring and careful execution."

The stories we've shared demonstrate how tax-loss harvesting can work alongside other retirement strategies to create better overall results. From the Thompsons' coordination with their retirement income planning to the Martinez family's systematic approach to market volatility, each family found ways to turn investment losses into tax advantages.

"The key," Sarah Chen reminds us, "is understanding that tax-loss harvesting isn't about changing your investment strategy to create losses. It's about making the most of natural market movements while staying focused on your long-term goals."

Michael Thompson offers a final perspective from his experience: "Once you understand the basic rules and set up a system to track everything, tax-loss harvesting becomes just another tool in your retirement planning toolkit. The tax savings we've generated have helped fund other important goals, including our grandchildren's education."

Looking Ahead

Speaking of education, our next chapter explores how 529 plans can create tax advantages while helping fund education expenses for children and grandchildren. The Williams' daughter Amy provides a perfect transition: "The money Mom and Dad saved through tax-loss harvesting helped them contribute more to our children's 529 plans. It's amazing how different tax strategies can work together to benefit the whole family."

Remember these key points as we move forward:

- Tax-loss harvesting requires attention to timing and careful documentation
- The wash sale rule needs constant monitoring
- Market volatility can create tax-saving opportunities
- Coordination with other strategies multiplies benefits
- Professional guidance helps optimize results

Turn the page to discover how 529 plans can add another dimension to your tax-efficient retirement strategy. As Jennifer Williams notes while reviewing her grandchildren's college savings statements, "Every tax dollar saved through smart investment moves can help secure the next generation's future."

References

Publication 550: Investment Income and Expenses

https://www.irs.gov/forms-pubs/about-publication-550

Publication 551: Basis of Assets

https://www.irs.gov/forms-pubs/about-publication-551

Jeff Weidner

CHAPTER 8: USE 529 PLANS TO HELP WITH GRANDCHILDREN'S EDUCATION

Understanding and Maximizing Education Savings Tax Benefits

What Is a 529 Plan?

A 529 plan, named after Section 529 of the Internal Revenue Code, is a powerful tax-advantaged savings vehicle designed specifically for education expenses. These plans work similarly to Roth IRAs, but for education instead of retirement. You contribute money after taxes, but all earnings grow tax-free when used for qualified education expenses. Additionally, many states offer tax deductions or credits for 529 plan contributions, creating immediate tax benefits for contributors.

The beauty of 529 plans lies in their flexibility. While originally designed for college expenses, these plans can now be used for K-12 private school tuition (up to $10,000 per year), apprenticeship programs, and even to repay student loans (up to $10,000 lifetime). This flexibility makes them an invaluable tool for grandparents looking to help with education while managing their own tax situation.

How 529 Plans Work

When you contribute to a 529 plan, you're essentially creating a tax-sheltered education investment account. The money you invest grows tax-free, and withdrawals remain tax-free when used for qualified education expenses. These expenses include tuition, books, supplies, computers, and room and board at eligible institutions.

One particularly valuable feature for grandparents is the ability to front-load contributions. You can contribute up to five years' worth of gift tax exclusions at once without triggering gift tax consequences. For 2024, this means a married couple could contribute up to $170,000 ($85,000 each) to each grandchild's 529 plan in a single year.

NOTE: 529 plans are a flexible and tax-advantaged way to help with your grandchildren's education, covering qualified expenses such as tuition, room and board, books, and supplies. They can also be used for K-12 tuition (up to $10,000 annually) and eligible apprenticeship programs. However, withdrawals from grandparent-owned 529 plans may impact financial aid eligibility, so consider strategies like transferring ownership to parents or delaying withdrawals until the student\u2019s final year of college. Additionally, starting in 2024, unused 529 funds can be rolled over into a Roth IRA for the beneficiary, with a lifetime limit of $35,000 and other restrictions. Consult a financial professional to maximize the benefits of your 529 plan.

The Impact on Financial Aid

Understanding how 529 plans affect financial aid has become increasingly important. Until recently, grandparent-owned 529 plans could potentially hurt a student's financial aid eligibility. However, recent changes to the FAFSA (Free Application for Federal Student Aid) have eliminated this concern, making grandparent-owned 529 plans more attractive than ever.

Now, let's see how real families are using these powerful education savings tools.

The Williams Family Strategy

Jennifer and Mark Williams sit at their dining room table, surrounded by college planning documents for their three grandchildren. "We always knew we wanted to help with college," Jennifer explains, "but we didn't realize how strategic we could be with the tax advantages until we really understood 529 plans."

State Tax Benefits: A Hidden Advantage

Before we continue with the Williams' story, it's important to understand how state tax benefits can significantly enhance your 529 plan strategy. Every state offers at least one 529 plan, but you're not limited to your own state's plan. You can invest in any state's plan regardless of where you live or where your grandchild might attend school.

Some states offer substantial tax deductions or credits for 529 plan contributions, but usually only if you invest in your home state's plan. Other states offer tax benefits regardless of which state's plan you choose. This variation in state tax treatment creates opportunities for strategic planning.

The Williams' Implementation Strategy

Jennifer Williams pulls out a spreadsheet showing their grandchildren's 529 accounts. "We discovered we could get state tax deductions for our contributions," she explains. "But what really caught our attention was the ability to front-load five years of gifts at once."

Mark adds his perspective: "We had just sold some investments at a gain, and our tax advisor showed us how front-loading 529 contributions could help offset our tax liability while jumpstarting our grandchildren's education funds."

Their approach involved careful coordination:

First, they researched different state plans. "We compared not just the tax benefits," Jennifer explains, "but also the investment options, fees, and track records of different plans. We wanted the best combination of benefits for both us and our grandchildren."

Then, they structured their contributions strategically. Instead of making equal contributions for each grandchild, they considered their different ages and needs. Their oldest grandchild, closer to college age, received more conservative investments, while their youngest grandchild's account took a more aggressive growth approach.

Investment Strategies Within 529 Plans

Understanding how to invest within 529 plans is crucial for maximizing their benefits. Most 529 plans offer age-based options that automatically become more conservative as the child approaches college age. They also typically offer static investment options that maintain the same allocation over time.

The Martinez family took a different approach with their grandchildren's 529 plans. "We chose individual fund options rather than age-based portfolios," Elena explains from their home office. "This gave us more control over the investment mix, allowing us to coordinate it with our other investment strategies."

Richard adds an important insight: "We learned that you can only change investment options twice per calendar year in a 529 plan. This made our initial investment choices particularly important."

Maximizing Control While Giving

One aspect of 529 plans that particularly appeals to grandparents is the level of control they maintain over the assets. Unlike direct gifts to grandchildren, 529 plans allow the account owner to maintain complete control of the funds. You can change beneficiaries, control the timing of distributions, and even take the money back if needed (though this would trigger taxes and penalties on earnings).

The Thompson family discovered the value of this flexibility when their oldest grandchild received a full academic scholarship. "We were initially concerned about having over-funded her 529 plan," Sarah Thompson explains from their living room. "Then we learned we could simply transfer the excess funds to our younger grandchild's account without any tax consequences."

Michael adds an important point: "Our advisor showed us that if we needed to withdraw the money for non-educational purposes, we'd only pay penalties on the earnings portion, not our original contributions. This gave us confidence to be more generous with our funding."

Navigating Qualified Expenses

Understanding what constitutes a qualified expense has become more complex as 529 plans have evolved. The definition now extends well beyond just college tuition and books. The Williams family keeps a detailed spreadsheet of qualified expenses to ensure they maximize the tax benefits.

"We were surprised by some of the things that qualify," Jennifer notes, reviewing their list. "Computer equipment, internet access, and even study abroad programs can be qualified expenses. But timing and documentation are crucial."

Their qualified expense tracking includes:

- Tuition and mandatory fees
- Books and supplies required for courses
- Technology needs for education
- Room and board (with specific limitations)

- Special needs equipment for students with disabilities

Coordinating with Other College Funding Sources

The Martinez family discovered the importance of coordinating 529 plan distributions with other forms of financial aid and education tax benefits. "We learned that timing our 529 plan distributions could affect our grandchildren's eligibility for other benefits," Elena explains.

Richard demonstrates their planning calendar: "We work closely with our children to understand what other resources are available. This helps us time our 529 plan distributions for maximum benefit."

The coordination involves understanding:

- How different tax credits interact with 529 plan distributions
- The optimal timing of withdrawals
- Which expenses to cover with 529 funds versus other sources
- How to document everything properly for tax purposes
- Building Educational Legacies Through Tax-Smart Planning

Looking out at their backyard where their grandchildren play, Mark and Jennifer Williams reflect on the impact of their 529 plan strategy. "What started as a tax-efficient way to help with education has become so much more," Jennifer shares. "We're not just saving for college – we're creating opportunities for generations to come."

The stories we've shared demonstrate the power of combining tax advantages with educational support. From the Thompsons' scholarship adaptation to the Martinez family's careful coordination of benefits, each family found ways to maximize both the tax advantages and educational impact of their 529 plans.

"The key," Sarah Chen reminds us, "is understanding that 529 plans are more than just savings accounts. They're flexible planning tools that can adapt to changing family circumstances while maintaining valuable tax benefits."

Elena Martinez offers a final perspective from her experience: "The tax savings are significant, but the real reward comes from knowing we're helping secure our grandchildren's future while managing our own retirement tax situation effectively."

Looking Ahead

As we move into our next chapter on the Augusta Rule, we'll explore another unique tax advantage that many retirees overlook – the ability to generate tax-free income from your home. The Williams' experience provides a perfect transition: "After maximizing our 529 plan contributions, we discovered we could use rental income from our home during major local events to generate additional funds for our grandchildren's education," Mark explains. "It's amazing how different tax strategies can work together."

Remember these key points as we proceed:

- 529 plans offer remarkable flexibility for education funding
- Careful coordination maximizes both tax and educational benefits
- Regular review and adjustment ensure optimal results
- Professional guidance helps navigate complex rules
- Integration with other strategies enhances overall outcomes

Turn the page to discover how the Augusta Rule can add another dimension to your tax-efficient retirement strategy. As Jennifer notes while booking their home for an upcoming local event, "Every tax-advantaged dollar we generate gives us more options for supporting our family's goals."

References

Publication 970: Tax Benefits for Education

https://www.irs.gov/forms-pubs/about-publication-970

Jeff Weidner

CHAPTER 9: UTILIZE THE AUGUSTA RULE FOR RENTAL INCOME

Understanding and Implementing Tax-Free Rental Income Strategies

What Is the Augusta Rule?

Named after Augusta, Georgia, home of the Masters Golf Tournament, the Augusta Rule (also known as Section 280A(g) of the Internal Revenue Code) provides a unique opportunity for homeowners to generate tax-free income. This rule allows you to rent your primary residence for up to 14 days each year without reporting the rental income on your tax return. What makes this rule particularly powerful is that there's no limit on how much you can earn during those 14 days – all of it remains tax-free.

The rule originated when Augusta residents began renting their homes to golf enthusiasts during the Masters Tournament. Congress recognized this practice and codified it into tax law, making it available to homeowners nationwide. Today, retirees can use this provision to generate significant tax-free income from their homes during local events, festivals, or business uses.

NOTE: The Augusta Rule allows homeowners to rent out their primary residence for up to 14 days per year without reporting the rental income, provided the property is rented at fair market value. This tax benefit is only applicable if the homeowner does not use the property as a rental business or deduct rental-related expenses. Ensure proper documentation, including rental agreements and proof of fair market value, to substantiate the claim. Misuse or lack of records can disqualify the tax-free benefit. Consult a tax professional to ensure compliance with IRS guidelines.

How the Augusta Rule Works

The mechanics of the Augusta Rule are straightforward, but precise documentation is crucial. You can rent your home for up to 14 days per calendar year, and the rental income is completely tax-free – you don't even need to report it on your tax return. However, if you rent for even one day more than 14 days, all rental income becomes taxable, and you must report everything you earned.

There's an important distinction between the Augusta Rule and regular rental property rules. Under normal circumstances, rental income is taxable, and you can deduct expenses like maintenance, utilities, and depreciation. With the Augusta Rule, while you don't pay taxes on the income, you also can't deduct any expenses related to the rental.

Strategic Applications

The Augusta Rule can be particularly valuable in several situations:

- Areas with major annual events (sports tournaments, festivals, conventions)
- Locations near universities (graduation weekends, homecoming)
- Business use of your home for meetings or events
- Popular tourist destinations during peak seasons
- Areas that host large corporate events

The Williams' Discovery

Mark and Jennifer Williams first learned about the Augusta Rule during a conversation with their tax advisor, Sarah Chen. "We live near the state fairgrounds," Jennifer explains from their well-maintained colonial home. "When Sarah mentioned we could rent our house during the state fair tax-free, we were intrigued but skeptical. It seemed too good to be true."

Implementing the Augusta Rule Successfully

The process of implementing the Augusta Rule requires careful planning and attention to detail. While the tax benefit is straightforward, the execution needs to be methodical to ensure compliance and maximize benefits.

Jennifer Williams opens her laptop, showing a detailed spreadsheet. "Our first step was identifying high-demand rental periods in our area," she explains. "The state fair was obvious, but we discovered several other opportunities we hadn't considered."

Their research revealed multiple rental opportunities:

- A major craft fair that draws thousands of visitors
- University parent weekends
- Regional business conferences
- Annual sporting events
- Holiday festivals

Mark adds an important insight: "What surprised us most was learning we could also use the rule when renting our home to our own business for meetings or events. This created another layer of tax planning opportunities."

Setting Fair Market Rent

One crucial aspect of the Augusta Rule is establishing a legitimate fair market rental rate. Sarah Chen explains this critical point: "The IRS expects the rental rate to be reasonable for your area and the event period. You need to document how you determined your rates."

The Martinez family approached this systematically when they began renting their home during their city's annual film festival. "We researched rates on various vacation rental websites," Elena explains from their kitchen table, pulling up local rental listings. "We documented comparable properties and rates during festival weeks to justify our pricing."

Richard adds practical advice: "We learned to track not just basic rental rates but also how prices changed during event periods. This helped us establish reasonable premium rates for high-demand times."

Documentation and Record Keeping

While the income may be tax-free, proper documentation remains essential. The Thompsons created a comprehensive system to track their Augusta Rule rentals after nearly making a costly mistake.

"We almost rented for a fifteenth day," Michael admits, showing their carefully organized rental calendar. "That would have made all our rental income taxable. Now we track everything meticulously."

Comprehensive record-keeping is essential for substantiating deductions and avoiding issues during an audit. **Best practices** include:

- Using accounting software to track income and expenses.
- Keeping digital and physical copies of receipts.
- Maintaining a mileage log for business vehicle use.
- Separating personal and business finances.
- Regularly reconciling records with bank statements.

Inadequate records may result in denied deductions or penalties during an audit. Document everything carefully.

Creating a Successful Rental System

Sarah Thompson shows us her rental management binder, organized with the precision she developed during her career as a corporate accountant. "When you're dealing with tax-free income, you want ironclad documentation in case of an audit," she explains. "We track everything from inquiry dates to final cleaning."

Their system includes several essential elements that other retirees can adopt. Beyond basic rental agreements, they maintain detailed records of:

"We photograph the house before and after each rental," Michael demonstrates, pulling up files on his tablet. "This not only protects us but helps track the condition of everything over time." They also keep careful notes about each guest's stay, which helps them improve their offering while maintaining clear records of actual rental days.

Business Use Applications

The Williams discovered an additional advantage of the Augusta Rule when they learned about using their home for business purposes. Mark, who still runs his woodworking business we discussed earlier, found a creative application.

"I hold quarterly board meetings and annual planning sessions for my business," he explains, showing us his beautifully appointed home office and meeting space. "Instead of renting hotel conference rooms, my business rents our home. The business gets a deduction, and we get tax-free income."

Sarah Chen emphasizes the importance of proper documentation for business use: "When renting to your own business, you need to be especially careful with documentation. The rental rate must be fair market value, and you need to document actual business use of the space."

Insurance Considerations

The Martinez family learned about insurance requirements through experience. "Our regular homeowner's policy wasn't sufficient," Elena recalls. "We needed additional coverage for short-term rentals."

Their insurance strategy evolved to include:

- Short-term rental coverage
- Additional liability protection
- Personal property coverage
- Business use endorsements

"The key," Richard notes, "is being completely transparent with your insurance company about how you're using your home. The small additional cost of proper coverage is worth the protection it provides."

Making the Augusta Rule Work for Your Retirement

Sitting on their back porch after their latest successful rental during the state fair, Mark and Jennifer Williams reflect on how far they've come with their Augusta Rule strategy. "What started as a simple idea to earn some extra tax-free income has become an integral part of our retirement plan," Jennifer shares. "The income helps fund our grandchildren's 529 plans and supports our charitable giving goals."

The experiences we've shared demonstrate the power of this often-overlooked tax provision. From the Thompsons' meticulous documentation system to the Martinez family's insurance strategy and the Williams' business application, each family found ways to maximize the benefits of the Augusta Rule while maintaining compliance with all requirements.

"The beauty of the Augusta Rule," Sarah Chen observes, "is its simplicity once you understand the boundaries. Fourteen days is fourteen days – no more, no less. Within that framework, retirees can create significant tax-free income opportunities."

Michael Thompson offers a final perspective from his experience: "The key is treating it like a business, even though it's tax-free income. Proper documentation, insurance, and attention to detail make all the difference."

Looking Ahead

As we move into our next chapter about deducting travel expenses for part-time work or consulting, we'll explore how retirees can turn necessary business travel into tax advantages. The Williams' experience provides a perfect transition: "After successfully managing our home rentals, we realized we could also be strategic about travel expenses related to Mark's woodworking business," Jennifer explains. "It's amazing how different tax strategies can complement each other."

Remember these key points as we proceed:

- The Augusta Rule offers valuable tax-free income opportunities
- Proper documentation is essential for success
- Insurance coverage must match your rental activities
- Business use creates additional planning opportunities
- Integration with other strategies enhances benefits

Turn the page to discover how business travel deductions can add another dimension to your tax-efficient retirement strategy. As Mark notes while planning his next woodworking trade show trip, "Understanding how to properly deduct business travel expenses has opened up new opportunities for combining business with pleasure while managing our tax situation effectively."

References

Publication 527: Residential Rental Property

https://www.irs.gov/forms-pubs/about-publication-527

Publication 925: Passive Activity and At-Risk Rules

https://www.irs.gov/forms-pubs/about-publication-925

CHAPTER 10: DEDUCT TRAVEL EXPENSES FOR PART-TIME WORK OR CONSULTING

Understanding and Maximizing Business Travel Deductions

THE BASICS OF BUSINESS TRAVEL DEDUCTIONS

For many retirees, part-time work or consulting provides both mental stimulation and additional income. When this work involves travel, understanding the tax implications can lead to significant deductions. Business travel deductions remain one of the most substantial tax benefits available to semi-retired professionals, but they also require careful attention to rules and documentation.

The IRS allows you to deduct ordinary and necessary travel expenses incurred while working away from your tax home. Your "tax home" isn't necessarily where you live – it's your regular place of business, regardless of where your family home is located. This distinction becomes important when structuring your travel deductions.

NOTE: To deduct travel expenses for part-time work or consulting, the travel must be directly related to your business, necessary, and reasonable in cost. Keep detailed records, including receipts, mileage logs, and the business purpose of the trip. Personal travel combined with business must be allocated, and only the business portion is deductible. Note that commuting expenses to your regular workplace are not deductible. Consult IRS guidelines or a tax professional to ensure compliance and proper documentation.

WHAT QUALIFIES AS BUSINESS TRAVEL?

Business travel deductions extend beyond just transportation costs. When you travel away from your tax home for business, you can potentially deduct:

- Transportation to and from your destination
- Lodging and meals
- Business communication costs
- Laundry and dry cleaning
- Tips related to business services
- Other ordinary and necessary expenses

However, the key to claiming these deductions lies in the primary purpose of your trip. If the primary purpose is business, you can deduct business-related expenses even if you combine the trip with some personal activities.

The Thompson's Experience

Michael Thompson discovered the value of business travel deductions when his woodworking business began attracting clients beyond his local area. "I was hesitant to take on projects that required travel," he admits from his workshop. "Then our tax advisor showed us how proper planning could make business travel both profitable and tax-efficient."

Mastering the Primary Purpose Test

Sarah Chen explains the crucial concept of primary purpose through Michael Thompson's experience. "When Michael started traveling to woodworking shows, he needed to understand how mixing business and pleasure would affect his deductions," she explains. "The key is documenting that business is the primary reason for the trip."

Michael pulls out his travel log, a detailed record of his recent trip to a major furniture show in North Carolina. "I spent four days at the trade show and added two personal days to visit family," he explains. "By understanding the rules, I knew exactly which expenses I could deduct and which were personal."

The primary purpose test isn't just about counting days. You need to show that you wouldn't have made the trip if not for the business purpose. Michael's documentation clearly demonstrates this through:

- Contracts or client meetings scheduled before travel
- Registration for trade shows or conferences
- Business correspondence showing the necessity of the trip
- Detailed daily logs of business activities
- Receipts clearly marked for business versus personal expenses

The Martinez Family's Consulting Strategy

Elena Martinez discovered new opportunities when she turned her gardening expertise into a consulting business. "I started getting requests to help design gardens in different climate zones," she shares from her home office. "This meant travel, but I needed to be smart about how I structured these trips."

Working with their tax advisor, Elena developed a system for maximizing the tax benefits of her consulting travel:

First, she ensures each trip has a clear business purpose documented before departure. "I learned to get everything in writing - the client's request, my proposal, and the agreed-upon scope of work," she explains.

Then, she maintains meticulous records of her daily activities. Her system includes photographs of client sites, detailed notes from meetings, and careful tracking of all expenses. "I use my phone to scan receipts immediately," she demonstrates. "Everything is organized by trip and client."

Making Business Travel Work in Retirement

Michael Thompson stands in his workshop, surrounded by pieces he acquired during his business travels. "What started as necessary trips to source unique materials has become an enjoyable part of semi-retirement," he reflects. "Understanding the tax rules has allowed us to make the most of every journey."

The stories we've shared demonstrate how thoughtful planning can transform business travel from a necessary expense into a tax-advantaged opportunity. From Elena Martinez's garden consulting adventures to the Thompsons' trade show strategies, each retiree found ways to combine business success with tax efficiency.

"The secret," Sarah Chen observes, "isn't just about knowing what you can deduct. It's about creating systems that make documentation automatic and audit-proof." She points to

Elena's digital receipt system and Michael's detailed travel logs as examples of best practices that make tax time easier while maximizing deductions.

Richard Martinez offers a final perspective from his own business travel experiences: "When you understand the rules and maintain proper documentation, business travel can open up new opportunities while providing valuable tax benefits."

Looking Ahead

As we move into our next chapter about Donor-Advised Funds, we'll explore how charitable giving can create another layer of tax advantages in retirement. The Williams' experience provides a perfect transition: "Our business travel exposed us to different communities and needs," Jennifer explains. "This inspired us to think more strategically about our charitable giving, leading us to discover the power of Donor-Advised Funds."

Remember these key points as we proceed:

- Business travel rules require careful attention to primary purpose
- Documentation systems ensure deduction success
- Technology can simplify record-keeping
- Proper planning maximizes tax benefits

- Integration with other strategies enhances overall results

Turn the page to discover how Donor-Advised Funds can add another dimension to your tax-efficient retirement strategy. As Mark notes while planning their charitable giving budget, "Just as we learned to be strategic with business travel, we've discovered how to make our charitable giving more impactful through smart tax planning."

After all, as Elena reminds us while booking her next consulting trip, "Every tax-efficient strategy we master gives us more resources to support the causes we care about while maintaining our retirement lifestyle."

References

Publication 463: Travel, Gift, and Car Expenses

https://www.irs.gov/forms-pubs/about-publication-463

Publication 535: Business Expenses

https://www.irs.gov/forms-pubs/guide-to-business-expense-resources

Jeff Weidner

CHAPTER 11: START A DONOR-ADVISED FUND FOR LEGACY GIVING

Understanding and Maximizing Charitable Tax Benefits

What Is a Donor-Advised Fund?

A Donor-Advised Fund (DAF) represents one of the most powerful and flexible tools for charitable giving in retirement. Think of it as a charitable investment account created for the sole purpose of supporting charitable organizations you care about. When you contribute to a DAF, you receive an immediate tax deduction, but you can take your time deciding which charities will receive grants from the fund.

This unique structure offers several key advantages. First, you can contribute during high-income years to maximize tax benefits, then distribute the money to charities over time. Second, you can contribute appreciated assets, avoiding capital gains taxes while receiving a deduction for the full market value. Third, the money in your DAF grows tax-free, potentially increasing the amount available for charitable giving.

How Donor-Advised Funds Work

When you establish a DAF, you make an irrevocable contribution to the sponsoring organization, which legally controls the funds. However, you retain "advisory privileges" that allow you to:

- Recommend grants to qualified charities
- Choose how the money is invested
- Name successor advisors to continue your legacy
- Create a giving strategy that spans generations

The Williams' Discovery of DAFs came at a perfect time. "We had just sold some highly appreciated stock from Mark's former employer," Jennifer explains from their living room. "We wanted to support several local charities, but we also needed time to research and plan our giving carefully."

NOTE: A Donor-Advised Fund (DAF) allows you to make charitable contributions, receive an immediate tax deduction, and recommend grants to charities over time. Contributions can include cash, stocks, or other appreciated assets, offering potential tax advantages like avoiding capital gains taxes. Ensure donations go to qualified 501(c)(3) organizations to maintain tax benefits. While funds can grow tax-free, they cannot be reclaimed for personal use. Consult with a financial advisor to align your DAF strategy with your legacy and tax planning goals.

Strategic Timing of Contributions

The Williams' situation illustrates one of the most powerful aspects of DAFs. Mark pulls up their tax records on his laptop: "We had a significant capital gain from selling company stock I'd held for over 20 years. Our advisor showed us how contributing some of those shares directly to a DAF would create multiple tax benefits."

Sarah Chen explains the strategy: "By contributing appreciated stock to their DAF instead of selling it first, the Williams avoided capital gains tax on the appreciation. They also received a tax deduction for the full market value of the shares. It's like getting two tax benefits from one contribution."

This timing strategy proved particularly valuable because they were in a higher tax bracket that year. Jennifer adds, "We knew our tax rate would be lower in retirement, so making the charitable contribution while we were in a higher bracket maximized our tax benefit."

Creating a Family Legacy

The Martinez family discovered that DAFs could help teach their children and grandchildren about charitable giving.

"We wanted to involve our whole family in philanthropy," Elena explains, showing a scrapbook of their charitable activities. "The DAF became a tool for family discussions about giving."

Their approach includes:

- Regular family meetings to discuss charitable goals
- Research projects for grandchildren to learn about different causes
- Collaborative decision-making about grants
- Documentation of the impact their giving creates

Richard notes an important benefit: "By naming our children as successor advisors to the DAF, we're creating a legacy of giving that will continue beyond our lifetime."

Investment Strategies Within DAFs

The Thompson's experience highlights the importance of investment planning within a DAF. "We realized the money we contributed could grow tax-free," Michael explains, reviewing their DAF's investment performance. "This meant we could potentially give more to charity over time."

Sarah shares their investment approach: "They worked with their DAF sponsor to create an investment strategy aligned with their giving timeline. Money needed for immediate grants stayed in conservative investments, while funds for future giving took a more growth-oriented approach."

Coordinating DAFs with Other Retirement Strategies

The Williams found that their DAF worked synergistically with other retirement tax strategies. "Our required minimum distributions became a perfect funding source for our charitable giving," Jennifer explains from their home office. "We discovered we could direct qualified charitable distributions from our IRAs to complement our DAF giving strategy."

Mark demonstrates their coordination approach using a carefully organized spreadsheet: "We map out our giving plans alongside our other retirement income sources. This helps us optimize both our charitable impact and our tax situation."

Their integrated strategy considers:

- Timing of RMDs and other retirement income
- Capital gains from investment sales
- Social Security taxation
- Medicare premium thresholds
- State tax implications

Selecting the Right DAF Sponsor

The Martinez family spent considerable time researching different DAF sponsors before making their choice. "We discovered that not all DAF providers are the same," Elena shares. "Different sponsors offer different investment options, minimum contribution requirements, and grant-making policies."

Richard explains their selection criteria: "We looked at several key factors:

- Minimum initial contribution requirements
- Ongoing contribution minimums
- Investment options available
- Grant-making requirements and processes
- Administrative fees
- Online access and ease of use
- Support services provided"

"What really helped us decide," Elena adds, "was talking with other families about their experiences with different sponsors. Personal recommendations gave us insights we couldn't get from marketing materials alone."

Managing Grants and Impact

The Thompsons developed a systematic approach to managing their charitable grants. "We wanted to make sure our giving had real impact," Sarah Thompson explains, showing their grant tracking system. "It's not just about giving money; it's about making a meaningful difference."

Michael demonstrates their process: "We research each organization carefully before making grants. We look at their financial health, their programs' effectiveness, and their alignment with our giving goals."

Their grant management system includes:

- Annual giving goals and priorities
- Research on potential grant recipients
- Documentation of grant impact
- Follow-up with organizations
- Records of all distributions

Building a Lasting Charitable Legacy

The concept of legacy giving took on new meaning for the Williams family when they started involving their adult children in their DAF decisions. "We realized we weren't just creating a charitable fund; we were establishing a family tradition of giving," Jennifer reflects, showing a photo album of family volunteer days at local charities they support through their DAF.

Mark explains their approach to legacy planning: "We set up regular family meetings to discuss our charitable giving. Each family member, including our teenage grandchildren, researches and presents charitable causes they think deserve support."

This family involvement has multiple benefits:

- Teaching financial responsibility to younger generations
- Creating shared family values around giving
- Developing research and presentation skills
- Building family bonds through shared purpose
- Establishing a lasting charitable legacy

Maximizing Tax Benefits Through Careful Planning

Sarah Chen explains how the Martinez family optimized their DAF contributions for maximum tax benefit: "Elena and Richard had several highly appreciated stock positions from Richard's years in corporate management. By carefully selecting which shares to donate, they maximized their tax savings while maintaining their desired investment allocation."

Elena shares their strategy: "We work closely with our financial advisor to identify which securities will provide the greatest tax benefit when donated. Sometimes these are stocks we'd like to reduce in our portfolio anyway, so it serves multiple purposes."

Their systematic approach includes:

- Quarterly review of appreciated securities
- Analysis of tax lots for optimal donation selection
- Coordination with overall portfolio rebalancing
- Integration with retirement income planning
- Regular tax projection updates

Measuring and Monitoring Impact

The Thompsons developed a unique system for tracking the impact of their DAF grants. "We wanted to know our giving was making a real difference," Michael explains, opening a carefully organized digital folder of impact reports from their grant recipients.

Sarah Thompson adds: "We created what we call our 'Impact Dashboard' that helps us see the collective results of our giving across different causes and organizations."

Their impact tracking includes:

- Specific metrics from each organization
- Stories and photos from funded programs
- Annual impact summaries
- Long-term tracking of supported initiatives
- Feedback from grant recipients
- Creating Impact Through Strategic Giving

As the sun sets through the windows of their family room, Mark and Jennifer Williams review their latest DAF impact reports. "What started as a tax-efficient way to give to charity has become so much more," Jennifer reflects. "We've created a family tradition that will outlive us."

The stories we've shared demonstrate the power of combining tax-efficient giving with purposeful family legacy planning. From the Martinez family's careful security selection to the Thompsons' impact tracking system, each family found ways to maximize both the tax benefits and the charitable impact of their Donor-Advised Funds.

"The beauty of DAFs," Sarah Chen observes, "lies in their flexibility. You can contribute when it's most tax-advantageous, invest for growth, and distribute grants thoughtfully over time. It's a powerful tool for both tax planning and charitable impact."

Elena Martinez offers a final perspective from her family's experience: "Our DAF has become the heart of our family's giving strategy. The tax benefits are significant, but the real value comes from bringing our family together around shared charitable goals."

Looking Ahead

As we move into our final chapter, we'll explore how to bring all these strategies together into a cohesive retirement tax plan. The Williams' experience provides a perfect transition: "Each strategy we've learned about, from the Augusta Rule to our DAF, plays a specific role in our overall tax planning," Mark explains. "The key is understanding how they work together."

Remember these key points as we proceed:

- DAFs offer powerful tax advantages for charitable giving
- Family involvement creates lasting impact
- Strategic timing maximizes tax benefits
- Careful investment management grows charitable resources
- Regular monitoring ensures meaningful impact

Turn the page to discover how to integrate all the strategies we've discussed into a comprehensive retirement tax plan.

As Jennifer notes while reviewing their family's charitable giving goals, "Every tax-efficient strategy we've mastered allows us to do more for the causes we care about while maintaining our retirement lifestyle."

After all, as Richard Martinez reminds us during their family's charitable giving meeting, "The most valuable legacy we can leave isn't just financial - it's teaching future generations how to manage resources wisely while making a positive impact on the world."

References

Publication 526: Charitable Contributions

https://www.irs.gov/forms-pubs/about-publication-526

Publication 561: Determining the Value of Donated Property

https://www.irs.gov/forms-pubs/about-publication-561

CHAPTER 12: CREATING YOUR COMPREHENSIVE TAX STRATEGY

Bringing It All Together

The Power of Integration

Throughout this book, we've explored numerous strategies for optimizing your tax situation in retirement. From Fixed Indexed Annuities to Donor-Advised Funds, each approach offers specific advantages. However, the real power comes from understanding how these strategies work together to create a comprehensive tax management system.

The Williams family demonstrates this integrated approach perfectly. "When we first started retirement planning," Jennifer explains from their home office, surrounded by carefully organized financial documents, "we thought of each strategy as separate. Now we understand how they complement each other."

NOTE: A comprehensive tax strategy should integrate all aspects of your financial plan, including income, investments, retirement accounts, and estate planning. Start by identifying your long-term goals and evaluating your current tax situation. Utilize strategies like Roth conversions, tax-loss harvesting, and charitable giving to minimize tax liabilities and maximize savings. Regularly review and adjust your plan as tax laws change or your financial circumstances evolve. Work with a qualified tax professional to ensure your strategy is tailored to your unique needs and stays compliant with current regulations.

Building Your Strategic Framework

Sarah Chen shares her approach to helping retirees create comprehensive tax strategies: "Think of tax planning like building a house. You need a solid foundation, strong supporting walls, and a protective roof. Each strategy we've discussed serves a specific purpose in your overall financial structure."

Let's look at how our families have layered these strategies:

The Foundation: Income Management

Mark Williams explains their base layer: "We started with understanding how to manage our regular retirement income through strategic Roth conversions and Fixed Indexed Annuities. This created the foundation for everything else."

Supporting Strategies: Tax-Efficient Growth

"Once we had our income foundation," Jennifer adds, "we looked at growth strategies like Opportunity Zones and tax-loss harvesting. These helped us build on our base while managing tax implications."

Protection Strategies: Risk Management

Elena Martinez shares their approach: "We used strategies like HSAs and the Augusta Rule to create additional tax-free income streams. This added flexibility and security to our plan."

The Synergy of Combined Strategies

The Thompson family discovered that certain strategies naturally complement each other. Michael opens his tax planning notebook, pointing to a diagram he's created. "We found that our business travel deductions paired perfectly with our Opportunity Zone investments. When visiting potential investment properties, we could properly deduct the travel costs through our consulting business."

Sarah Thompson adds, "And our HSA strategy works hand in hand with our retirement income planning. By maximizing HSA contributions during our higher-income years, we created tax-free funds for healthcare while managing our tax brackets."

Creating Income Layers

The Martinez family developed what they call their "Tax-Efficient Income Pyramid." Richard explains their approach from their sunlit kitchen:

Base Layer: Guaranteed Income
"We started with Social Security and our Fixed Indexed Annuity income as our foundation," Elena explains. "This gives us predictable, partially tax-advantaged income we can count on."

Middle Layer: Flexible Income
Richard points to their planning documents: "Here we use a combination of Roth conversions, tax-loss harvesting, and strategic withdrawals from different accounts to manage our tax bracket."

Top Layer: Opportunistic Income
"This is where we incorporate the Augusta Rule, business consulting, and other variable income sources," Elena adds. "These give us flexibility while maintaining tax efficiency."

Family Legacy Integration

The Williams found ways to combine multiple strategies for enhanced family benefits. "We use the tax savings from our various strategies to fund our grandchildren's education," Jennifer explains. "The money we save through tax-loss harvesting and the Augusta Rule often goes directly into their 529 plans."

Mark adds an important insight: "And our Donor-Advised Fund complements our family giving goals. We can time our contributions for maximum tax benefit while teaching our grandchildren about charitable giving."

Timing and Coordination

Sarah Chen emphasizes the importance of timing when combining multiple strategies. "Success comes from understanding not just how strategies work together, but when to implement each one," she explains, showing a timeline she created for the Thompson family.

Michael Thompson demonstrates their coordination approach: "We create an annual tax strategy calendar that maps out key decisions and actions." Their calendar includes:

First Quarter Focus:
"We review our HSA contributions and plan any Roth conversions," Sarah Thompson explains. "This gives us the full year to adjust if needed."

Mid-Year Assessment:
"Summer is when we implement most of our Augusta Rule rentals during local events," Michael adds. "We also review our tax-loss harvesting opportunities."

Year-End Planning:
"The final quarter is crucial for coordinating charitable giving through our DAF with any tax-loss harvesting or Opportunity Zone investments," Sarah notes.

Technology and Tracking

The Martinez family developed sophisticated tracking systems to manage their multiple strategies. "With so many moving parts, we needed a way to see everything clearly," Elena explains, showing their digital dashboard.

Richard demonstrates their tracking system: "We use software to monitor:

- Income from various sources
- Tax bracket positioning

- Strategy implementation timelines
- Documentation requirements
- Results and adjustments needed"

Professional Coordination

The Williams emphasize the importance of having a coordinated professional team. "Each strategy requires specific expertise," Jennifer explains. "The key is having professionals who communicate with each other."

Their professional team includes:

- Tax advisor for overall strategy
- Financial planner for investment coordination
- Estate attorney for legacy planning
- Insurance specialist for risk management
- Business consultant for entrepreneurial ventures

Mark adds: "Regular team meetings ensure everyone understands how their piece fits into the larger picture."

Adapting to Change

The Thompson family learned the importance of building flexibility into their tax strategy. "Tax laws change, family situations evolve, and market conditions shift," Michael explains from his home office. "Our plan needed to be adaptable."

Sarah Thompson shares their approach to maintaining flexibility: "We regularly review each strategy's effectiveness and make adjustments as needed. Last year, when the markets were volatile, we increased our focus on tax-loss harvesting while temporarily reducing our Opportunity Zone investments."

Teaching the Next Generation

The Williams discovered that their comprehensive tax strategy created valuable teaching opportunities for their children and grandchildren. "We're not just managing taxes," Jennifer explains. "We're teaching our family how to think strategically about money."

Their educational approach includes:

- Monthly family financial discussions
- Hands-on experience with business operations
- Involvement in charitable giving decisions
- Understanding of tax-efficient wealth transfer
- Long-term legacy planning

Creating Sustainable Success

Elena Martinez emphasizes the importance of sustainability in tax planning. "These strategies only work if you can maintain them long-term," she explains while reviewing their family's quarterly results. "We focus on approaches we can consistently execute year after year."

Richard adds insight from their experience: "It's about finding the right balance between maximizing tax benefits and maintaining a manageable system. We learned to start with a few core strategies and gradually add more as we became comfortable."

Their sustainable approach focuses on:

- Regular strategy reviews
- Simplified documentation systems
- Clear division of responsibilities
- Manageable implementation timelines
- Consistent professional oversight
- Building Your Tax-Efficient Future

As the sun sets on our exploration of retirement tax strategies, the Williams family gathers in their living room for their monthly financial review. "Looking back," Jennifer reflects, "it's amazing how these different strategies have come together to transform our retirement."

Mark nods in agreement, gesturing to their financial documents spread across the coffee table. "What started as individual tax-saving ideas has become a comprehensive system that benefits our whole family. Each strategy strengthens the others."

The experiences we've shared throughout this book demonstrate the power of integrated tax planning. From the Thompsons' business and investment coordination to the Martinez family's sustainable approach, each family found ways to combine multiple strategies into a cohesive whole that serves their unique needs.

Key Lessons from Our Journey

As Sarah Chen reminds us, successful retirement tax planning requires attention to several critical elements:

Integration
"Every strategy we've discussed works better when coordinated with others," she explains. "Tax-loss harvesting supports charitable giving through DAFs. The Augusta Rule provides funding for 529 plans. HSAs complement retirement income planning. It's all connected."

Flexibility

The Martinez family's experience shows us the importance of adaptability. "Tax laws change, family needs evolve, and market conditions shift," Elena notes. "Success comes from building flexible systems that can adapt to change while maintaining their tax efficiency."

Documentation

Michael Thompson emphasizes the importance of proper record-keeping: "Whether it's business travel expenses or Augusta Rule rentals, documentation protects your tax benefits and makes implementation easier."

Family Involvement

"Perhaps the most rewarding aspect," Jennifer Williams shares, "has been watching our children and grandchildren learn these strategies. We're creating a legacy of financial wisdom that will benefit generations to come."

Looking to Your Future

As you implement these strategies in your own retirement planning, remember:

- Start with your foundation - understanding and optimizing your basic retirement income sources.
- Add complementary strategies gradually, mastering each one before moving to the next.
- Build strong documentation systems from the beginning.
- Maintain a coordinated professional team.
- Involve family members to create lasting impact.

The Path Forward

The tools and strategies we've explored provide a framework for tax-efficient retirement living. As Richard Martinez reminds us, "The goal isn't just to save taxes – it's to create more resources for what matters most: supporting our family, contributing to our community, and enjoying the retirement we've worked hard to achieve."

Mark Williams offers a final perspective from their years of implementing these strategies: "Each small step in tax efficiency compounds over time. Start where you are, implement what you can, and keep building your knowledge and systems. The results will surprise you."

As we close this book, remember that your journey to tax-efficient retirement is just beginning. Take these strategies, adapt them to your situation, and create your own success story. After all, as Jennifer Williams notes while scheduling their next family financial meeting, "The most valuable legacy we can leave is showing future generations how to manage wealth wisely while making a positive impact on the world."

References
Publication 17: Your Federal Income Tax

https://www.irs.gov/forms-pubs/about-publication-17

TCJA: Tax Reform Basics for Individuals and Families **https://www.irs.gov/newsroom/tax-reform-resources**

CONCLUSION: BUILDING YOUR TAX-EFFICIENT RETIREMENT

Putting It All Together

Throughout this book, we've explored thirteen powerful strategies for creating a tax-efficient retirement. From Fixed Indexed Annuities to Donor-Advised Funds, each approach offers unique advantages. However, as our families have demonstrated, the real power comes from understanding how these strategies work together to create a comprehensive tax management system.

The Building Blocks of Tax-Efficient Retirement

The Williams family's journey illustrates how different strategies can complement each other. "When we first started," Jennifer explains from their home office, "we thought of each strategy as separate. Now we see how they create a complete picture."

Their integrated approach includes:

Income Management

- Strategic use of Fixed Indexed Annuities
- Careful coordination of retirement account withdrawals
- Thoughtful timing of Social Security benefits
- Tax-efficient investment approaches

Wealth Preservation

- Health Savings Accounts for medical expenses
- Tax-loss harvesting for investment efficiency
- Opportunity Zone investments for tax-advantaged growth
- Strategic use of the Augusta Rule

Legacy Creation

- 529 plans for education funding
- Donor-Advised Funds for charitable impact
- Business strategies for family involvement
- Coordinated estate planning

Real-World Implementation

The Thompson family's experience demonstrates the importance of systematic implementation. "We learned to start with the basics and gradually add more sophisticated strategies," Michael shares. "Each new approach built on what we had already mastered."

Sarah Chen emphasizes the value of professional coordination: "Success comes from having experts who understand how different strategies interact. Your tax advisor, financial planner, and attorney need to work together toward your goals."

Creating Your Personal Strategy

The Martinez family's methodical approach to implementing tax strategies provides a valuable template for other retirees. "We created what we call our Strategy Integration Timeline," Elena explains, showing a carefully organized planning document. "It helped us prioritize which strategies to implement first and how to build on them over time."

Their approach breaks down into manageable phases:

First Phase: Foundation Building

"We started with the basics," Richard explains. "Understanding our retirement income sources, optimizing Social Security timing, and establishing proper documentation systems. This created a strong foundation for everything else."

Second Phase: Tax-Efficient Growth

Elena continues: "Once we had our foundation, we added strategies like HSAs and tax-loss harvesting. These helped us manage current taxes while building for the future."

Third Phase: Legacy Development

"Finally, we incorporated more advanced strategies like our Donor-Advised Fund and Opportunity Zone investments," Richard adds. "These aligned with our longer-term family and charitable goals."

Keys to Success

Through our families' experiences, several crucial elements for success have emerged:

Proper Documentation

The Williams family's meticulous record-keeping system demonstrates the importance of documentation. "Every strategy requires its own type of documentation," Jennifer notes. "Having organized systems makes everything easier at tax time."

Professional Guidance

Sarah Chen emphasizes the role of professional advice: "These strategies are powerful but complex. Working with qualified professionals helps you avoid costly mistakes and maximize benefits."

Family Communication

"Perhaps our most valuable lesson," Mark Williams shares, "was learning to involve our entire family in the process. Regular family meetings keep everyone informed and engaged in our long-term planning."

Regular Review and Adjustment

The Thompsons' quarterly strategy reviews highlight the importance of monitoring and adapting. "Tax laws change, family situations evolve, and market conditions shift," Michael explains. "Regular reviews help us stay on track and adjust as needed."

Taking Action: Your Next Steps

The success stories we've shared demonstrate that implementing tax-efficient strategies doesn't happen overnight. As Sarah Chen advises, "Start with clear priorities and build systematically."

Step 1: Assessment
Begin where the Williams family started - with a comprehensive review of your current situation:

- List all retirement income sources
- Review existing tax strategies
- Identify immediate opportunities
- Document current financial goals

"Understanding where you are is essential before deciding where to go," Jennifer explains. "We spent a full month just organizing our financial information before implementing any new strategies."

Step 2: Strategy Selection
The Martinez family's methodical approach shows how to choose which strategies to implement first:

- Focus on strategies that align with your immediate needs
- Start with simpler approaches before moving to more complex ones
- Consider your comfort level with each strategy
- Evaluate required resources and commitments

Step 3: Building Your Team
Michael Thompson emphasizes the importance of professional support: "Having the right team makes all the

difference. Each member brings specific expertise that helps optimize your overall strategy."

Essential team members typically include:

- Tax advisor for strategy development
- Financial planner for investment coordination
- Estate attorney for legacy planning
- Insurance specialist for risk management

Step 4: Implementation Timeline

Elena Martinez shares their approach to timing: "Create a realistic timeline that allows you to master each strategy before adding new ones. We found that trying to do everything at once was overwhelming and ineffective."

Consider a phased approach:

- Months 1-3: Foundation strategies
- Months 4-6: Basic tax optimization
- Months 7-12: Advanced strategies
- Year 2: Integration and refinement

The Path to Long-Term Success

The Williams family's five-year journey demonstrates what successful implementation looks like over time. "Looking back," Mark reflects from their living room, surrounded by family photos, "our greatest success came from staying consistent and adapting as circumstances changed."

Jennifer adds, "Each year brought new opportunities and challenges. Having a flexible system helped us adjust while maintaining our tax efficiency."

Key Elements for Lasting Success:

Regular Review Cycles

The Thompsons established a rhythm for reviewing their strategies:

- Monthly check-ins for basic tracking
- Quarterly reviews of strategy performance
- Annual comprehensive planning sessions
- Ongoing professional consultations

"These regular reviews help us stay proactive rather than reactive," Michael explains. "We can spot opportunities and address challenges before they become problems."

Continuous Learning

Elena Martinez emphasizes the importance of staying informed: "Tax laws change, new strategies emerge, and family needs evolve. We make learning a priority."

Their approach includes:

- Regular meetings with professional advisors
- Subscription to tax and financial updates
- Family education sessions
- Sharing lessons learned with others

Creating Your Legacy

Perhaps the most inspiring outcome from our families' experiences is the impact on future generations. "What started as tax planning has become a family legacy," Richard Martinez shares. "Our children and grandchildren are learning valuable lessons about financial stewardship."

The Williams family now holds monthly financial education sessions with their grandchildren. "We're not just teaching them about taxes," Jennifer explains. "We're showing them how to think strategically about money and create positive impact in their communities."

Final Thoughts

As we conclude our exploration of tax-efficient retirement strategies, remember that success comes from consistent application of sound principles. The families we've followed demonstrate that while the strategies may be sophisticated, the path to implementation is straightforward:

- Start with clear goals
- Build systematically
- Maintain proper documentation
- Work with qualified professionals
- Involve family members
- Stay flexible and adaptive

Sarah Chen offers this final perspective: "The most successful retirees aren't necessarily those who use every available strategy. They're the ones who carefully choose and implement strategies that align with their values and goals."

Mark Williams shares a final thought as he reviews their family's progress: "Every journey toward tax efficiency begins with a single step. Take that step, keep learning, and stay committed to your goals. The results will amaze you."

Remember, the strategies we've explored aren't just about saving taxes – they're about creating more resources for what matters most in your retirement years: supporting your family, contributing to your community, and enjoying the life you've worked hard to build.

As you close this book and begin your own journey toward tax-efficient retirement, take inspiration from these families' experiences. Your path may be different, but the principles remain the same. With careful planning, consistent execution, and proper guidance, you too can create a tax-efficient retirement that benefits both your family and your future.

Additional Important References Throughout:

Publication 590-A: Contributions to Individual Retirement Arrangements (IRAs)

https://www.irs.gov/forms-pubs/about-publication-590a

Publication 560: Retirement Plans for Small Business

https://www.irs.gov/forms-pubs/about-publication-560

Publication 936: Home Mortgage Interest Deduction

https://www.irs.gov/forms-pubs/about-publication-936

Publication 946: How to Depreciate Property

https://www.irs.gov/forms-pubs/about-publication-946

Note: IRS publications are regularly updated. When implementing these references, you should verify the most current versions and include the tax year relevant to each publication.

Jeff Weidner

GLOSSARY OF TERMS FOR SMART TAX STRATEGIES

Adjusted Gross Income (AGI)

Definition: AGI is your gross income minus specific deductions, such as student loan interest, IRA contributions, and health savings account (HSA) deductions. It serves as the basis for calculating taxable income.

Augusta Rule

Definition: This rule allows homeowners to rent out their primary residence for up to 14 days a year tax-free. Commonly used for short-term rentals or hosting events.

Backdoor Roth IRA

Definition: A strategy for high-income earners to contribute to a Roth IRA by first contributing to a traditional IRA and then converting it to a Roth IRA, bypassing income limits.

Capital Gains Tax

Definition: A tax on the profit from the sale of assets, such as stocks, real estate, or businesses. Long-term capital gains (held over a year) are taxed at lower rates than short-term gains.

Catch-Up Contribution

Definition: Additional contributions allowed for individuals aged 50 and older to retirement accounts like 401(k)s and IRAs, providing an opportunity to boost savings closer to retirement.

Donor-Advised Fund (DAF)

Definition: A charitable giving vehicle that allows individuals to make a charitable contribution, receive an immediate tax deduction, and recommend grants to charities over time.

Estate Tax

Definition: A tax on the transfer of assets from a deceased individual's estate to their beneficiaries, applicable if the estate's value exceeds a certain threshold.

Exclusion Ratio (Annuities)

Definition: The percentage of an annuity payment considered a return of principal and thus not taxable. The remainder of the payment is subject to income tax.

Fixed Indexed Annuity (FIA)

Definition: An insurance product that provides tax-deferred growth linked to a market index (like the S&P 500) while offering protection from market losses and options for lifetime income.

Gift Tax Exclusion

Definition: The annual limit per recipient that an individual can gift without incurring gift tax. For 2024, the exclusion amount is $17,000.

Health Savings Account (HSA)

Definition: A tax-advantaged account for individuals with high-deductible health plans. Contributions are tax-deductible, grow tax-free, and withdrawals for qualified medical expenses are also tax-free.

Income-Related Monthly Adjustment Amount (IRMAA)

Definition: An additional premium charged for Medicare Part B and Part D for individuals with higher income, based on their Modified Adjusted Gross Income (MAGI).

Marginal Tax Rate

Definition: The tax rate applied to your last dollar of taxable income, representing the rate at which additional income will be taxed.

Medicare Premium Surcharge

Definition: An increase in Medicare premiums for high-income earners, calculated using the Income-Related Monthly Adjustment Amount (IRMAA).

Modified Adjusted Gross Income (MAGI)

Definition: AGI adjusted by adding back certain deductions, such as student loan interest or tuition deductions, used to determine eligibility for certain tax benefits like Roth IRAs or IRMAA.

Opportunity Zones

Definition: Designated economically distressed areas where investors can receive tax advantages for investing in projects through Qualified Opportunity Funds (QOFs).

Qualified Charitable Distribution (QCD)

Definition: A direct transfer of funds from an IRA to a qualified charity, which can satisfy RMD requirements while excluding the distribution from taxable income.

Qualified Opportunity Fund (QOF)

Definition: An investment vehicle created to invest in Opportunity Zones, allowing investors to defer and potentially reduce capital gains taxes.

Required Minimum Distribution (RMD)

Definition: The minimum amount retirees must withdraw annually from their tax-deferred retirement accounts starting at a certain age, as mandated by the IRS.

Required Minimum Distribution Age (SECURE Act Adjustments)

Definition: The age at which RMDs must begin, adjusted under the SECURE Act to 73 for individuals born between 1951-1959 and 75 for those born in 1960 or later.

Roth Conversion

Definition: The process of transferring funds from a traditional IRA or 401(k) to a Roth IRA, paying taxes upfront in exchange for tax-free withdrawals in the future.

Sequence of Returns Risk

Definition: The risk that the timing of withdrawals from a retirement account will negatively impact overall savings due to poor market performance early in retirement.

Social Security Taxation

Definition: A portion of Social Security benefits may be subject to federal income tax if combined income exceeds certain thresholds.

Stretch IRA (Legacy Considerations)

Definition: A strategy (now limited by the SECURE Act) allowing non-spouse beneficiaries to "stretch" distributions from an inherited IRA over their lifetime, reducing annual tax burden.

Substantial Improvement Requirement (Opportunity Zones)

Definition: A rule requiring investors in Opportunity Zones to spend at least the purchase price of a property (excluding land value) on improvements within 30 months.

Tax-Advantaged Accounts

Definition: Accounts like IRAs, 401(k)s, HSAs, and Roth IRAs that offer tax benefits such as deferred or tax-free growth.

Tax-Deferred Account

Definition: A retirement account, such as a traditional IRA or 401(k), where contributions and earnings are tax-deferred until withdrawal.

Tax-Loss Harvesting

Definition: A strategy to offset capital gains by selling underperforming investments at a loss to reduce taxable income.

Tax Torpedo

Definition: A sudden increase in marginal tax rates caused by the taxation of Social Security benefits when other income crosses certain thresholds.

Triple Tax Advantage (HSA)

Definition: The unique tax benefit of HSAs, where contributions are tax-deductible, earnings grow tax-free, and withdrawals for qualified medical expenses are also tax-free.

Let me know if you'd like any definitions expanded or additional terms included!

For Additional Support:

We are here to help. Request your free Social Security Analysis and retirement Income Plan. If you would like personalized guidance in maximizing your Social Security benefits and creating a comprehensive retirement income strategy, please contact:

Boom Retirement Solutions

(888) 839-1611

SCAN TO SCHEDULE

AN APPOINTMENT

For a free copy of our other book "Maximizing Social Security Benefits" send an email to jeff@boomretirement.com and in the Subject Line write "Free Book Social Security."

Jeff Weidner

Made in the USA
Monee, IL
13 September 2026

62976606R00125